# Screw Firmly From Rear

## By Matthew Black

Readers outside the United Kingdom may wish to browse the Glossary of Terms at the back of this book, which explains a number of slang and colloquial terms used in the story.

# Chapter 1

It would have been hard to imagine a more idyllic location. The late summer sunshine was just starting to burn away a light mist that had formed in the early hours, and which was now hanging thinly over the clear waters of the small lake from which the Hidden Lake Sun Club took its name. A pair of blue tits hopped mischievously amongst the branches of the willow trees that lined the edge of the water, before darting across a small clearing to continue their game amongst the slender branches of a silver birch. Further from the water's edge a mallard slowly but determinedly made its way from one side of the lake to the other, barely disturbing the surface of the water as it went. But it was not the playful blue tits, nor the elegant mallard that elevated this tranquil scene from merely delightful to 'picture perfect'. For sitting atop a wooden stake that one of the club's members had risked life and limb to secure in place, a solitary kingfisher kept watch over the lake's clear waters, considering which of the many small fish swimming beneath to take for its breakfast.

It wasn't the first time that Gwen had seen the bird, but every sighting of the lake's resident kingfisher was something special, and today it was probably closer to her than it had ever been. Gwen kept perfectly still and watched while the kingfisher surveyed the living larder beneath the water's surface, seemingly unable to make up its mind where to strike first. However, when the kingfisher eventually left its perch it was not to secure itself a meal, but to find somewhere more private from which to go fishing. Disturbed by the sound of a door opening, the kingfisher dived off its stake and skimmed over the surface of water and out of sight, providing Gwen with the briefest of glimpses of its startlingly electric blue feathers. Just as the bird disappeared from sight Gwen heard a woman's voice issuing a greeting.

'Good morning Gwen.'

Gwen turned to see a tall young woman with long dark hair standing behind her, and wearing just a pair of flip flops and a light blue 'T' shirt that was several sizes too large for her but still barely covered her navel.

'Sorry about the nightwear,' she said. 'But it does get a bit chilly at night at this time of year and I don't like my shoulders to get cold. Mike's fine sleeping naked all year round and he never needs anything to keep himself warm, even on the coldest nights.'

'Good morning Michelle,' replied Gwen. She smiled 'Don't worry about the T shirt, I think it's rather pretty actually. I feel the cold too these days so I usually wear something at night, even if it is only a woolly hat and a pair of thick socks. Now then, I've got your sandwiches here.'

'How much do I owe you?' asked Michelle. 'In total.'

'That's £35 altogether,' replied Gwen, and she handed over a package carefully wrapped in tin foil.

'I know it's a bit of an extravagance, but your sandwiches have been absolutely delicious, and it's been so convenient for us just telling you want we want one day, and then having you deliver them to us the next morning. It's my holiday as well, after all, not just a week away from the office for Mike.'

'I'm so glad you liked them. Do you think you'll be coming back next year?'

Michelle pulled off her ill-fitting T shirt and folded it into a neat square, letting the warm morning sun bathe her body, and leaving her standing in just her flip-flops.

'Just you try and stop us Gwen. I only hope that we can get the same week, and that you'll still be running your sandwich service of course.'

'I hope I will too,' replied Gwen. 'But you really never know what's in store when you reach my age. I'm almost in my nineties now.'

'You're never!'

'It's true I'm afraid. I put my youthful zest for life down to a good diet, sensible shoes and the love of a good man, and that's despite his sometimes excessive level of activities in the bedroom department.'

'Lucky you,' said Michelle, a broad grin on her face. 'My Mike's fine in that respect but – well between you and me - a little bit more attention might be nice from time to time.'

'You can have too much of a good thing my dear, believe me. I've had to point that out to my George on many an occasion, particularly in the early years when he was in the Navy. Fortunately he was away overseas quite a lot, so at least I had a bit of time to catch my breath and prepare myself in readiness for the next onslaught.'

'He's a good man Gwen,' replied Michelle. 'And from what I've heard of him I'm sure he's only ever had eyes for you.'

'It wasn't his eyes I had to worry about my dear. His hands had plenty of practice with the ladies while he was away, and so I'm afraid to say did some of his other bits. He'd come home from some foreign port and I'd no idea where he'd been - metaphorically speaking or physically for that matter - so I used to confine him to the spare bedroom for a fortnight until any exotic infections he'd brought back with him had time to make their presence known, and I only let him get anywhere near me once he'd completed a course of antibiotics and had stopped scratching. He wasn't particularly happy with the situation of course, but it was his own fault.'

'Well I'm sure you did a wonderful job getting him on the straight and narrow eventually,' replied Michelle, mouthing platitudes but wondering just what the hell George had been getting up to when he'd been away. 'Now, just let me go and get your money.'

Michelle turned away and walked towards the log cabin that had served as her holiday home from home for the last seven days. She was gone barely a minute before emerging back into the sunshine clutching her purse but still wearing nothing other than her flips flops.

'Here you are Gwen. Thirty five I think you said.' She handed Gwen three crisp £10 notes and five £1 coins. 'We've really loved staying here. The cabin's got everything we needed for a great holiday, and everybody's been really friendly. It's been smashing, and a week's decent weather has been an added bonus.'

Gwen smiled again. Her son Bradley had been largely responsible for the Hidden Lake Club getting planning permission to put a log cabin on its land, so with that and her fledgling sandwich business she had far more than a passing interest in the success of the club's log cabin as a naturist holiday retreat.

'Perhaps next year I'll be a bit more adventurous and try something from your 'Premier' selection,' Michelle said as she shut her purse. 'But it's much too easy to stick with what you know. That said, pilchard and peanut butter does sound a rather unusual combination.'

'I can guarantee you'll never have tasted anything quite like it,' replied Gwen, still smiling. 'My George adores it.'

'I'm sure. On second thoughts perhaps I'll try your special BLT. You can't really go wrong with Bacon, Lettuce and Tomato.'

'Actually Michelle that's my special Banana, Lard and Tuna.'

Gwen's suggestion for a 'Premier' BLT substitute went unheard as two swans disturbed the silence and started a noisy territorial dispute over a tatty pile of sticks at the water's edge.

'It's such a beautiful spot,' said Michelle as she gazed across the lake. 'Particularly on a lovely, warm summer's day.'

Gwen nodded her head and agreed with her new friend that it was indeed a beautiful spot. Such a beautiful spot, in fact, that Gwen had already decided it should also serve as her final resting place.

'I would like my ashes scattered on the lake just there,' she said, pointing to a spot close to where the kingfisher had been sitting just a few minutes earlier. 'When my time comes.'

'I'm sure it'll be a good while yet,' replied Michelle, squinting in the bright sunlight and trying to figure out roughly where Gwen had meant.

'I hope so dear, I really do, but I suppose I'll just have to wait and see what Mother Nature has in store for me.'

# Chapter 2

The Hidden Lake Sun Club's first Executive Committee meeting of the New Year appeared destined to carry on from where the last one of the old year had left off. If that proved to be the case it would be an unusual occurrence, but the Committee's members had spent most of the last meeting arguing about just two topics, and those same two topics appeared destined to get the new year off to a similarly acrimonious start as the end of the old one. With no specific time for the committee meeting to end, its members' bickering seemed set to continue until the first of them decided they'd had enough and got up to go home, at which point the others would no doubt have attributed blame for the evening's lack of harmony on him or her. Fortunately before that situation had arisen at the previous meeting the Committee had managed to agree that - in the season of peace and goodwill – they would call a truce with a view to resuming hostilities the following January. The following January had now arrived and with it an imminent recommencement of battle. And so it was that the two items on the month's agenda – being the same as the last – were those of the Club's finances and its membership. Trivial matters, such as holes in the club's car park and the truly appalling state of the gentlemen's lavatorium one Sunday morning early last November could wait until much closer to the start of the new summer season. So it was perhaps not surprising that when Derek Hobbs - the Club's reluctant Treasurer - Chairman Geoffrey Harris, and the Membership, Social, and Sports Secretaries - Anna Dixon, Louise Simmons and Alison Hopkins respectively -convened in the Hidden Lake's clubhouse, that the windows of the building were very soon steamed up from the volume of hot air being generated.

'Now then Derek,' began Geoffrey, immediately putting the club's Treasurer in the firing line. 'Let me recap where we left off before Christmas. You put the membership subscription up in order to attract additional income, and we actually received significantly less. That is correct, is it not?'

Derek said nothing but waved the index finger on his left hand back and forth.

'So do you have an explanation for that particular outcome, other than you cocked up?'

'Well as I understand it,' replied Derek. 'The decline in income was not as a direct result of members not renewing their membership – and Anna will no doubt attempt to correct me if I'm wrong, or indeed if I'm right – but of changing their membership status in an attempt to save money.'

'And avoid the bog cleaning rota,' added Alison.

'Quite possibly.'

'You don't think the introduction of the new three-tier membership system might have confused some of our less cerebral members by any chance? I mean, 'Gold', 'Silver' and 'Bronze' would seem to be quite easily understood, but more than one of our brethren initially thought that it meant the depth of their suntan – 'Silver' being the lightest, 'Gold' the middle and 'Bronze' the deepest.'

'I can't account for all our friends, but no, I don't think they would have been too confused. After all, the status and benefits for each of the three levels were quite clearly spelt out in the Club's newsletter, on an email, and pinned up in the clubhouse.'

'You are of course working on the rash assumption that they actually read one or the other,' said Alison. 'Just remind me what they are again?'

Anna sighed. "Bronze' membership – this was supposed to be a 'no-frills' level for new members who pay the lowest fee. It was deliberately kept at a fairly modest level to keep them coming here, and to try and prevent them from wandering off to other nearby clubs. They don't have to clean the bogs either.'

'There aren't any near here,' said Geoffrey.

'Bogs?' asked Derek.

'Clubs. The closest is just over twenty miles away, so that's hardly near.'

'It might be near enough to attract those who live anywhere between the two clubs, so a low fee was intended to provide an incentive to keep the buggers coming here and not going over there. 'Bronze' members pay a fee each time they visit, so those 'Bronze' members who visit more frequently would be better off paying for 'Silver' membership which would allow them unlimited access. 'Silver' members are also excluded from the bog cleaning rota. 'Gold' members, on the other hand, get the same unlimited access as 'Silver' members but also unlimited camping rights for the summer season. 'Silver' members can also camp if a spare pitch is available, but they pay a fee per day each time they camp. So..'

'So 'Silver' members who camp regularly would be better off paying for 'Gold' membership,' suggested Geoffrey. 'But on the down side they also get lumbered with the toilet cleaning duties.'

'You got it.'

'So are you seriously telling us the deciding factor comes down to how much it's worth not to have to clean the toilets?' asked Alison, who appeared to be developing an aversion to the idea and potentially contemplating down-grading her own status and that of her partner Steve to 'Silver'.

'Well frankly if you'd seen the state of the men's swamp the other week you could well believe it,' replied Anna. 'How is it that a man can tap a golf ball into a hole from six yards but can miss a urinal from six inches?'

'Well it wasn't me then,' laughed Derek. 'I can't get that close, except on a very cold day.'

'Anyway Derek,' said Geoffrey, who was keen to get the meeting back on track and avoid a detailed analysis of the relative merits of the three-tiered membership system just in case there was any correlation with 'Gold' members changing their membership in order to avoid toilet cleaning duties. 'The bottom line is that we put the cost of membership up and received less income as a result.'

'Something like that,' replied Derek.

'You should have foreseen that happening,' said Anna. 'After all, there's some law or other about that sort of thing, isn't there?'

There was a brief silence before Alison decided that the unwelcome outcome of Derek's decision to increase membership subscriptions could be explained by physics.

'Newton's Third Law,' she said. 'That's it. Sir Isaac Newton's Third Law. It says that for every action there is an equal and opposite reaction.'

Despite this pronouncement Anna wasn't convinced.

'Are you sure about that? I always thought that was something to do with people knocking balls together.'

'Were you thinking of anybody's balls in particular?' asked Derek. He laughed. 'Because if it's Brad's that would explain a lot. The poor old bugger. Fancy ending up having a permanent limp.'

'Is he taking any medication for that yet?' asked Louise. 'I only ask because the last I heard Leanne was trying to sort it out all by herself, but unfortunately she'd started developing muscles in her forearm that Popeye would be proud of. And all to no avail, or so I've heard.'

Derek shook his head. 'I've no idea. I'd heard from someone or other that he'd been to see his doctor, who said there's nothing physically wrong with him - in that department at least, so his inability to get it ...'

'I think we get the picture, now *please* can we get back to the agenda,' said Geoffrey, but without managing to stop Derek from continuing his explanation of Brad's condition.

'..suitably firm appears to be psychosomatic or some kind of strange syndrome.'

'Well it's not Stiff-Man Syndrome that's for sure,' said Alison, unsuccessfully trying not to laugh, and nearly wetting herself in the process.

'You're having us on,' replied Anna once Alison had composed herself and discretely checked her knickers for laughter-induced leakages. 'Stiff-Man Syndrome indeed, what a load of old nonsense.

But Alison wasn't to be denied telling her story. 'I'm not having you on, honestly I'm not. Stiff-Man Syndrome is a very rare neurological condition where the patient gets muscle spasms which can be triggered by sudden noises or even by being touched. I remember Brad telling me about it a while ago. He was playing miniten at the time, and one of his opponents had just served three straight aces. Without thinking I jokingly shouted out something about him having 'Stiff Man' syndrome and he threw his racquet down on the ground, and then stormed across the court and swore at me. After the match he apologised for his behaviour and I apologised for the joke, hopefully without letting on that I knew about his little problem. Actually, it's a bit ironic when you think about it, given his condition. It's also a bit ironic that it's mostly women who get it, which is why it's usually known these days as 'Stiff-Person Syndrome' rather than 'Stiff-Man'. Anyway, Brad told me that he knew about it because somebody had objected to a planning application he was dealing with on the basis that any sudden noise from the builders and the poor bloke would turn into a tablet of stone.'

Geoffrey gave Alison a look that should have told her that the Chairman was supposed to be in control of the meeting, but when that failed he decided to try and bring it to order more diplomatically.

'Thank you Alison. I'm sure that's all very enlightening, and we've certainly all learnt something new this evening. Now I'll ask again. Can we *please* get back to business?'

'We were discussing whether the fall in subscriptions as a result of Derek's decision to put up the membership fee accorded with Newton's Third Law,' replied Alison, wiping tears of laughter away from her eyes.

'So we were,' replied Anna. 'Although those executive toys are probably a better example. You know, the ones where you let a ball drop against a row of balls all suspended in a line, and when that ball hits the ball next to it the ball at the other end pops up. It looks a bit like magic but I'm sure it isn't really because there's no such thing. Is there?'

'I think it's the Law of Diminishing Returns,' suggested Alison. 'And nothing to do with Newton banging his balls together. For example, putting insulation in your loft reduces your heating bills, and putting more insulation in will reduce your bills further. But if you keep putting in more insulation you'll get to a point..'

'Where you can't get into your loft,' replied Anna. 'No, it's not that. I think it's just a case of Sod's Law.'

'Silly Old Sod's Law, more like,' muttered Louise.

'I've got it,' replied Alison, leaping to her feet. 'It's the Law of Unintended Consequences. That's it. You do something, and it causes something else to happen which you weren't expecting. In our case it happened to be something we didn't want, which was a bit unfortunate really. Derek put up the fees and the unintended consequence was that our membership dropped. So there you are: Q-E-D.'

'You mean a bit like a butterfly flapping its wings and causing a tsunami?' suggested Anna.

'No Anna, that's Chaos Theory I think. Isn't it?'

Whether the club's financial shortfall could be attributed to chaos theory, or just chaos within its Committee was probably immaterial. Whatever theory the Committee members eventually decided upon the simple fact was that they would probably end up blaming Derek who, in an age-old management technique practiced throughout the country and oft-referred to as 'Crapping on from a great height', tried to shift the blame to anybody other than those present.

'I have to say the reduction in fiscal reserves this year has been largely due to the way Brad handled our application for planning permission to re-build the clubhouse which resulted - as I'm sure you are all aware - not only in permission to rebuild the clubhouse, but to station that log cabin down by the lake.'

'Now that would be the same log cabin that's been continuously occupied by paying visitors all last summer, which should more than pay for itself inside five years, and following which should return us a healthy profit,' replied Geoffrey, slightly irritated at Derek's obvious attempt to divert blame from himself.

'Yes, it is. And you're right about the long-term prospects, but in the short-term it's having a detrimental effect on our cash-flow.'

'Well, it shouldn't be,' replied Alison. 'Finance for the log cabin should have been provided for out of the Club's *capital* account, not revenue. The Club has got two accounts Derek, hasn't it?'

'We've got.. Well, we've got a bank account with some money in it so let's leave it at that, shall we?'

'You're not standing for re-election as Treasurer are you. That's not a question by the way.'

Derek's tenuous track of the Club's finances had been a long-standing concern for several of the Committee members, but now was not the time to get involved in an argument about it, because blame was clearly the name of today's game, and Anna was pretty sure she'd seen some writing on the clubhouse wall which said 'Watch your arse.'

'Well at this point in the proceedings some of those amongst us may decide that our woes are actually due to my inability to recruit a sufficient number of new members, and not due to that twat ...' She pointed to Derek. 'Screwing up big time. So..'

'Whoa, calm down Anna,' interrupted Alison, well aware that her friend's single use of a mild four letter expletive could be a precursor to a full-blown pre-menstrual rant where every third word could well begin with the letters F and U.

'So on that basis I'm making a suggestion. Derek can have my job as Membership Secretary and I'll look after the money. And then we'll see which is the easier. After all Derek, it's not easy to convince a sceptical general public that social nudity is about getting closer to nature and respecting each other as individuals, and is nothing to do with sex, let alone getting them to try it for themselves and then paying for the privilege if they want to join a club. *That* Derek, is difficult - bloody difficult in fact. All you have to do is take their money and try, if you can, not to lose it.'

There was a brief silence, during which Anna wiped away a dribble of saliva from her chin with the back of her hand, and then glared at each of the Committee members in turn. Then, before Anna could direct her vitriol to anyone else Geoffrey spoke.

'I understand how you feel Anna. But I'm sure it's not all any one person's fault. The Committee voted on the new membership scheme so in that respect I suppose we're all equally to blame. The question is – what do we do about it?'

'Well I suppose we could increase the fee for renting our log cabin' suggested Louise. 'After all, it's very popular, and our visitors are always telling me it's in such a lovely spot down by the lake. The trees seem to make it all the more secluded and far-removed from the hustle and bustle of daily life. Gwen even told me there's a kingfisher down there from time to time, although I've never seen it myself.'

Despite what seemed like a sensible suggestion Geoffrey wasted no time in dismissing it out of hand. 'We checked the prices of accommodation against other clubs, so I think that putting our charges up would only result in fewer bookings. We're back to that Newton's Chaotic Law of Diminishing Consequences the Third, or whatever we eventually agreed it was.'

'Well in that case there's only one thing we can do' suggested Alison. 'And that's to go out and recruit some new members.'

Anna rolled her eyes. 'And how *exactly* are you proposing we achieve that? If it was that easy don't you think we'd be up to our eyeballs in prospective members?'

Alison knew her friend was right, and bearing in mind how close Anna appeared to be to throwing a full-blown paddy, decided to pour a little oil on troubled waters.

'I know you've worked really hard Anna and you've done everything you possibly could, but I think there is a way.'

'Oh yeah, and like – *how* exactly?'

'Poach them.'

'I beg your pardon?' said Geoffrey. 'Did I hear you say 'poach them'?'

'Yes you certainly did. Because that, ladies and gentlemen – and Derek at a pinch – is the only way we are going to get the new members we need. Look - you said it yourself – there aren't any other clubs near here. But we all know other naturists who drive virtually past our door to get to their clubs, and then there are the others who don't belong to a club but go to the monthly swim and sauna at Barnsted House. Think about it for a moment - Louisa and Ken Higgins live about five miles away from here but belong to Westlands which is about another twenty miles. Then there's Mike and Nikki Smith who drive about twenty five miles in the opposite direction - almost past our door in fact. And why do they do that? I'll tell you why. Habit, that's why. They've always belonged to the same club and they know the people there. They're just reluctant to change, that's all. They're reluctant to change in the same way that Derek was reluctant to change his gas supplier. So what..'

'Yes, and I still haven't got any bloody heating,' complained Derek, before Alison had a chance to finish what she was saying.

'Alright, so that's a bad example, but can you see what I mean? What you need to do, Anna, is put on the charm the next time you go to the Barnsted House swim, and get some of those people up here.'

'And *how* am I supposed to do that?' replied Anna, clearly unimpressed by the idea of what was essentially theft as far as she was concerned, and possibly even constituted people trafficking.

'Well you could offer them a couple of free day visits in the summer, and in the meantime invite them to one of our evening socials. It's not as if we don't know the people, and they know quite a few of us as well. So it really shouldn't be too difficult.'

Even if Anna wasn't at all keen on the idea it was clear that Louise saw the potential.

'It's an idea I suppose,' she said. 'We could do with a few more people at some of the winter functions. I know, why don't you try and get them to come along to the Valentine's night disco. That's always a good do, and with a few extra people, well, who knows what it might do for our membership. What do you the rest of you think?'

There were general mumblings about 'protocol' and 'etiquette', and how it wasn't the done thing to poach other clubs members before the assembled group eventually reached the general consensus that it was actually a bloody good idea, and why had nobody thought of it before.

'Leanne might even find herself a new Mr Right,' muttered Anna, under her breath. 'And by God wouldn't she be grateful, especially if he'd got a more interesting type of Stiff-Man Syndrome.'

# Chapter 3

Neither Brad nor Leanne knew exactly what time it was when the phone in their lounge rang because the batteries in the bedside clock appeared to have died about two hours earlier. It was certainly something after two o'clock in the morning as identified by the motionless timepiece, and also before seven because it was still pitch dark outside. On that basis if the caller was either Gwen or George then the call was likely –but not necessarily - to be urgent and needed to be answered. If, on the other hand, the caller claimed to be a Nigerian prince wishing to advise Brad or Leanne that he had a large number of US Dollars that required a temporary home in exchange for a modest advance or the PIN number for their debit card then they could go and get stuffed. As it turned out the voice Brad heard once he'd crawled out of bed, made his way to the lounge and spluttered the words 'Hello, Brad speaking' was that of his mother, thereby avoiding the need for him to pass the handset to Leanne who had a most effective line in abusive greetings, especially at that time in the morning.

'Hello dear. Kissee kissee. Just a quick call so there's nothing to worry about.'

'Do you know what time it is Mother?'

'No, but then time depends on precisely whereabouts in the world you are Bradley my dear. And in any event some say that time itself is just a mere concept, and that we are all living in a parallel Universe. They also say that one day the Universe will collapse into a giant black hole and then come out the other side where everything that's ever happened will happen again but backwards this time. Eventually it'll reach the point at which everything was created, and then it'll all disappear with the reverse of whatever a big bang is. I haven't told George any of this because I really don't want to worry him unduly, so I'd be grateful if you don't mention it either.'

Brad could well imagine that one or two of his family did indeed spend a significant proportion of their time in a parallel Universe, but now was really not the time to engage his mother in a debate about general relativity, because she'd almost certainly win what would inevitably turn into a war of attrition.

'Maybe, but the last time I looked we were both in England, and as usual at this time of the year it's perishing cold and our heating's not on yet, so what is it you want to tell me?'

'I just need to let you know how important our family is to your father and me.'

Brad sighed. His mother was either being her usual decidedly eccentric self or had been drinking, or possibly both. It was becoming increasingly difficult to tell these days, although she wasn't slurring her words so alcohol was probably nothing more than an aggravating factor. On the plus side Gwen hadn't felt it necessary to engage Brad in a prolonged exchange of passwords or other security details before she was prepared to talk to him. That, in itself, was a relief because Gwen's unorthodox method of preventing identity theft could easily result in a preamble far longer than the subsequent conversation.

'Who is it?' shouted a voice from the bedroom.

'It's Mother.'

'Oh, it *is*, is it? I might have guessed. Well unless it *really* can't wait until tomorrow just tell her to fuck off and come back to bed.'

Brad had no hesitation in ignoring his wife's profane demands, although he would have appreciated her suggesting a diplomatic way of dealing with an unwanted caller at this time of night. Fortunately Gwen didn't hear her daughter-in-law, and began justifying the reason for her untimely call.

'So I thought to myself '*Why not phone up my favourite son*'..'

'Your only son' interrupted Brad, more than slightly irritated at having been disturbed at such an unearthly hour for what appeared to be nothing more than a bit of a social chit-chat.

'… and wish him a very happy New Year, and tell him how much I love him.'

'That's very sweet of you Mother, but it's probably about four o'clock in the morning, it's the middle of January, and I've got to get up and go to work in maybe just a couple of hours' time, so I'm afraid your timing leaves more than a little to be desired.'

'That's as maybe dear, that's as maybe. But better late than never, that's what I say. You hear these terrible stories about people not telling their loved ones how much they care about them, and before they know it they've been run over by a bus and it's too late. I am of course talking *metaphorical* buses you understand, because I know how infrequent rural services are these days. So the chances of you actually being run over or even hit by a real bus are probably fairly slim. I expect it's far more likely that you'd be hit by a car, or a juggernaut with foreign licence plates, a horsebox, or even a tractor around these parts -

but that's not what people say is it? No, they don't. They say they've been run over by a bus. Well, they don't actually say *they've* been run over obviously, but I think you get my drift. The point is it would be so sad if anything were to happen to either of us and I hadn't had a chance to tell you how much I love you and your sister, and her children Jeremy and Zena.'

'Jeffrey and Tina. Their names are Jeffrey and Tina.'

'Are you sure about that?'

'Yes Mother, absolutely.'

'Oh well, Jeffrey and Tina it is then. It'd be so sad if I didn't let them know how I..'

There was a brief pause before Gwen addressed her dialogue to another individual entirely.

'No George. Not there. I've told you before about doing that. Now stop it immediately.'

There was another brief pause, causing Brad to listen intently, if unintentionally.

'I really don't care if Mrs Ramsbottom does let her husband do it George - not that I believe for one minute that she would bearing in mind she used to teach at Sunday school. I'm not letting you and that's final. Now take it away from there at once.'

Brad didn't care to speculate on what his father was up to, but he had a damn good idea, and he also knew that Leanne would have squeezed his balls until they imploded if he'd ever dared to try it with her. That said, given Brad's on-going malfunction of a rather personal nature Leanne would probably not have objected to Brad's overtures too vehemently, provided that she could divert his attention to another more receptive part of her anatomy.

'Honestly Bradley. Your father - I really don't know what gets into him sometimes. Most men his age can't even remember what to *do* with it, let alone get it in that disgraceful state.'

Brad wasn't entirely sure what his mother was referring to by 'that disgraceful state' but got a pretty good idea when he heard George complain loudly about Gwen slapping him on the bell end.

'Well just you keep it to yourself. I'm trying to have a civilised conversation with your only son, and you keep waving that thing about the place and poking it where it isn't wanted. I *know* it's very impressive George –you've told me that dozens of times - but *please* just put it back inside your pyjamas out of harm's way before it gets cold.'

Brad could just about make out a low murmur which he took to be his father issuing a grudging acceptance of Gwen's demands.

'Thank you darling, that's much better. I do like your pyjamas to be nice and tidy. Maybe we'll play with it tomorrow, and if you're a very good boy until then we'll do that thing you like with the whipped cream and glace cherries.'

Brad could just about make out his father asking whether the thing with the whipped cream and glace cherries could also involve the fur-lined handcuffs and blindfold, to which Gwen replied that it would depend on how George behaved between now and then, and that she'd have to think about it.

'Right dear, that's sorted your father out. Well, got him under control anyway. Now then, what was I saying before he tried to put his..'

'Well you started off by saying you wanted to wish me a happy New Year and then you started going on about how you wanted to make sure you told Zara and me that you love us before we get run over by an infrequently running rural bus' said Brad, before Gwen had a chance to give her son an unwanted account of George's attempted manoeuvres.

'Oh yes, so I was. Right then, here we go. 'Happy New Year' Bradley my dear. I'm assuming it's not your birthday in the next couple of weeks, but if it is I'd like to wish you many happy returns at the same time to save money on another phone call. May the coming year bring you and your dear sister Zara good health, wealth and much happiness. I'm not including that wretched woman of yours – she whose name shall never pass my lips, even if I could remember what it is and I can't - as I'm sure you realise.'

Brad hadn't even bothered to wonder if his mother's long-running contempt for his wife was about to show any signs of mellowing, and it clearly wasn't, so he didn't feel inclined to take her bait.

'No Mother, I didn't think you'd be including Leanne in your seasonal greetings because you never do, and I don't believe you ever have. So, now that's all done I'd just like to say I'm giving you all my love too. Now *please*, can I get back to bed?'

'In a minute dear, in a minute. Now then, as I was saying..'

But Gwen didn't say anything, certainly not that she intended Brad to hear. Instead she just whispered 'Oh, *George*.'

'Mother?'

'Sorry dear, I got a bit distracted. Your father was just..just..oh *George*. Yes, just there. No, up a bit. A bit more. And a bit more. That's it, just *there*. Now then, gently. No, a little bit harder. That's it. Oh *George*. Oh, yes. Oh, you are a naughty boy George. I suppose now you've got that far you want to carry on, don't you? Yes, I thought you might. You are a *naughty* old bugger George, you really are.'

Brad knew neither what to do, say or think. His first reaction was to put down the phone and leave his parents to get on with it – and Brad didn't care to ponder on precisely what 'it' might have been, opting simply for leaving them to get on with what was clearly a most private business. But whether Brad's reluctance to slam the handset down and terminate what was rapidly becoming a disturbing surrogate for live phone sex was due to inherent good manners or a subconscious reaction to his only previous experience of the genre was something he didn't care to ponder. Even as his parents were becoming pre-occupied with something more interesting than a late night phone call to their only son, Brad's thoughts returned to a phone call he'd made from an ancient red public phone box in the late 1980s. That one phone call had already cost him well over a fiver before he even got to hear the words 'soft inner thigh', whispered by a husky female who called herself 'Giselle' and promised of untold pleasures to come if Brad only shoved some more money into her hot telephony slot. He hadn't been on the phone to 'Giselle' more than a couple of minutes - or so it seemed - before a succession of rapid pips in his ear had alerted him to the fact that his erotic fantasies were about to be unceremoniously terminated unless he replenished his credit. Unfortunately the warning came at precisely the same as time as Giselle started to whisper what she wanted to do with Brad's big, hot man-thing if he stayed on the phone line for just a few minutes more. The timing was probably co-incidental, but suggested more than a hint of collusion between Giselle and the telephone company, both of whom appeared intent on relieving Brad of still more of his hard-earned cash. Brad hadn't had time to consider whether or not the expenditure of several more Pounds would result in Giselle disclosing her innermost secrets – but on the basis that a fiver had got Brad absolutely bugger all in the way of titillating entertainment so far it should have been a clear no-brainer.

Despite the inevitability of throwing good money after bad, Brad had started delving frantically in his trouser pockets in an attempt to find enough loose change to meet the insatiable demands of both Giselle and of the company holding the rights to the premium rate phone number. He had just managed to retrieve a coin from the screwed-up remnants of a paper tissue in his right-hand trouser pocket with his left hand – daring not to change the hand with which he was grasping the phone's handset lest he should cut off Giselle in her prime and be compelled to start another expensive phone call from the very beginning – and was about to give himself another minute or so of heavy breathing time when he heard a loud knocking on the door of the phone box.

'I say. You. Yes, you. Young man.'

Brad turned his head and saw an elderly woman outside the telephone box holding a walking stick in one hand and a Spaniel on a lead in the other. She was beating the door of the telephone box with her walking stick, which was clearly the more effective of her two options.

'Yes, you. Are you going to be much longer in there? I've been waiting an absolute age already. Other people want to use that telephone box as well as you.'

The woman stared through the telephone box's panelled glass door and in the general direction of Brad's crotch.

'What are you *doing* in there anyway?'

Distracted from the task of trying to maintain contact with Giselle, Brad dropped the coin onto the floor of the telephone box where it rolled into a corner before gluing itself down courtesy of the remnants of a half-chewed fruit gum. There was a further sharp tap on the telephone box door.

'I hope you're not doing what I think you're doing.'

'Do you want me to undo my suspender belt and slip off my skimpy white panties sweetheart?' murmured Giselle, just as Brad decided to risk stooping over to try and retrieve what he had originally thought was a fifty pence piece, but on closer inspection turned out to be a low denomination coin from a country somewhere in sub-Saharan Africa wrapped in tin foil. Unfortunately for Brad confirmation that his only remaining small change was of insufficient value to allow time for Giselle to say anything more substantial than 'luscious firm breasts' came only after he'd picked the coin up and discovered the quality of well chewed fruit gums as a form of impromptu adhesive.

'It's disgusting, that's what it is,' said the elderly woman to two others who had joined her and were forming the beginnings of a short queue. 'You should be ashamed of yourself, you should. Doing sort of thing that in there. You should go to the bathroom if you need to.'

Brad didn't immediately respond to the reprimand, but waved his hand around in an unsuccessful attempt to dislodge the errant fruit gum. Then he started pushing against the door of the telephone box with his backside until it was ajar.

'Sorry,' he said, raising his voice so that the three assembled women could all hear through the gap between the door and its frame. 'I'm just trying to get all this sticky stuff off my hand and then I'll be finished.'

'Oh you dirty little pervert,' shouted the woman with the Spaniel on a lead 'I thought you were just having a tiddle in there.'

'No, I..'

'I know just what you were up to,' shouted the woman, and began banging the door with her stick once again, causing the Spaniel to start barking. Brad realised he was going to have one hell of a job explaining that he was entirely innocent of any improper behaviour, apart from exercising a previously latent curiosity about the content of premium rate phone services.

'You randy little devil!' exclaimed Giselle, having come to her own conclusion regarding Brad's current state of affairs, and chiding herself for not employing some delaying tactics. 'I know I'm red hot stuff but that was seriously quick!'

'No, you don't understand.'

'Oh I do honey, I do. Don't worry. Hope you enjoyed it. Remember to call me again the next time you need it really badly, won't you? Jiz-hell by name, Jiz-heaven by nature. Ta ta sweetheart.'

With an apparently well satisfied customer Giselle put down the phone ready to take the next punter's call, leaving Brad standing in the phone box with the telephone handset in one hand, and a half-masticated fruit gum attached to the other.

\*\*\*

It had taken a lot of explaining and more than a humble apology for the length of time they had been kept waiting before the three women outside the phone box eventually accepted that Brad's behaviour could be explained by him being mildly inquisitive and a bit odd, and not some kind of pervert as they had originally concluded. Brad had toyed with the idea of simply walking away from the scene and leaving his accusers to 'tut tut' away to themselves, but discounted that idea on the basis that the three of them were leaning against the door of the phone box and effectively incarcerating him, a situation Brad was concerned might continue until the police arrived. Fortunately for him, Brad managed to persuade his captors that he would never be tempted to urinate in a telephone box, let alone do anything else of a more private nature, and that he'd simply been on the phone to a friend of unspecified gender or age. Had he been aware that 'Giselle' was only slightly younger than his mother, and - far from wearing a peek-a-boo bra, white stockings, suspenders and high heels as she had claimed - was actually clad in a badly-fitting, ancient grey tracksuit and cheap trainers from a sweatshop in Bangladesh – Brad would never have made that ill-fated phone call. In fact he wouldn't have called her if he'd known that Giselle's boudoir was located in nothing more exotic than a one-bed Council flat on the thirteenth floor of a concrete tower block in north London, that her next door neighbours had been busted for intent to supply

Class A substances, or that the two broken lifts to the aforesaid tower block had well over a pint of lager piss sloshing around in them. But that was all in the distant past, and since then Brad had taken no part in any form of telephonic sexual activity other than to blow Leanne a kiss or two down the phone when he'd been away from home on business overnight, and she'd demanded that he call her from his hotel at ten o'clock sharp to prove that he wasn't out on the town enjoying himself.

And so it was that Brad's current situation – holding on the phone waiting for his mother to either (a) let him know that she'd call him back later, or (b) resist an unanticipated liaison with George and continuing her conversation with her son – had brought back deeply disturbing images that had convinced him that sex, telephones and elderly women were a combination to be avoided if at all possible. In fact any two from the three were probably best avoided, especially if the elderly woman was his mother.

His memories of that fateful day fresh in his mind, Brad was brought back to his senses by what sounding like china breaking on a hard surface, immediately followed by his parents shouting. Gwen may or may not still have been holding the telephone's handset, but Brad clearly heard his father's voice over that of his mother.

'Oh bugger that hurt!'

'Mother,' responded Brad, almost instinctively. 'Are you alright Mother? What's happened?'

'I'm fine dear. Your father just knocked a vase of roses off the coffee table and it send all my little china nick-nacks scattering. Now he's gone and scratched his leg into the bargain.'

'On the coffee table?'

'No dear, on the roses. He was trying to get his leg over.'

'I don't need to know the details if you don't mind Mother,' replied Brad, rather wondering what his father had been up to for the last ten minutes if he'd only just got around to attempting a definitive move.

'No, you don't understand dear. He said he wanted to try something a bit different, and was trying to get his leg over the coffee table when he caught it on my best vase. He's broken it too. My vase that is, in case you were wondering. The coffee table's fine.'

Despite Brad having told his mother he didn't want to know the details, he now found himself in possession of more information than he could cope with at any time of day let alone at silly o'clock in the morning. Unfortunately Gwen didn't appear to feel the need to finish her conversation with Brad before reconvening her liaison with George.

'Your father really is quite *remarkable* for his age you know Bradley. For any age in fact. So I don't really feel I should try and dissuade him from his more *base* instincts for as long as he feels he's up to it, and provided he doesn't do himself any mischief. After all, I…Oh *George*, that really is *gorgeous*. Oh yes, don't stop now. *Oh yes George!*'

With George clearly well on the way to achieving something or other - even if it hadn't been exactly what he'd been attempting – he and Gwen both became silent, and all Brad could make out over the phone line was a slow, rhythmic squeaking as one of the legs of the coffee table objected to the combined weight of the two octogenarians. Once again Brad found himself in the highly unenviable situation of being on the wrong end of a phone whilst a close encounter of the humping kind appeared to be taking place at the other, and was just about to put the phone down when Gwen spoke. Unfortunately it wasn't to him.

'Oh *yes*, George. *Yes George, yes, yes, yes!*'

It was no good. Brad decided it was time to put the phone down and leave his mother and father to get on with it. It was sometime between two and seven o'clock in the bloody morning, and here he was standing in the freezing cold listening to his parents behaving like a couple of sex-mad seventeen year olds on skunk.

'Goodnight Mother, I'll call you tomorrow.'

Brad didn't expect his mother to respond, and his words went unheard as Gwen began descending from the climactic experience of the last couple of minutes and began chiding her errant husband once more.

'Oh, *now* look what you've gone and done George,' Brad heard his mother complaining. 'You can jolly well clear that up yourself.'

# Chapter 4

The following Saturday Brad and Leanne drove over to George and Gwen's modest bungalow for afternoon tea. Leanne had originally intended to find some excuse to avoid having to go, primarily because neither she nor Gwen would be able to find a kind word to say about the other, and secondly because Gwen's catering skills left a lot to be desired – like somebody to do it all for her. But despite having previously told Brad he could f'ing well go on his own if he really felt he must, Leanne eventually capitulated when Brad told her he'd take her out to dinner that evening if Gwen's sandwiches were, in her sole opinion, totally inedible. All things considered the strong likelihood of dinner *'Chez Juliette et Hugo'* was just too good to miss, and with Brad's sister and her partner Frank understood to be joining them for tea, there was also a rare but welcome opportunity to try and delve into their private lives. Unfortunately the second reason for Leanne changing her mind was only partly fulfilled, because when she and Brad arrived at his parents' bungalow George told them that Zara had to attend to some private business and would be joining them later, and that Frank was otherwise occupied.

'And she dropped her bloody kids off here first,' complained George as he finished explaining his daughter's proposed comings and goings. 'So your mother's told me I've got to mind my 'Ps' and 'Qs' which is a bit of a bugger all things considered. Still, that's what grandparents are for I suppose, looking after their damn kids' offspring. Anyway, I suppose now you're here you'd better come in.'

George led Brad and Leanne into the lounge where his grandson and granddaughter were sitting on the carpet amidst a pile of toys, books, crayons and pieces of paper. Gwen was nowhere to be seen.

'Right then, sit yourselves down,' he said.

Brad started to park his rear in an armchair next to the window until Leanne grabbed his arm and pulled him over to a settee which she'd already decided was where they were going to sit. Whether it was sitting on a comfy sofa or because the lounge was over-warm Brad had no idea, but almost as soon as his backside had hit a cushion he started to yawn.

'Busy on the job last night were you then?' asked George. 'Worn you out, has she?'

Brad didn't give Leanne the chance to make any snide comments, and immediately attributed his tiredness to being woken during the night by nuisance phone callers, of which his mother was the chief culprit.

'Oh yes, sorry about that,' replied George. 'I didn't realise you were still hanging on the phone while we were getting down to a bit of the old horizontal pairing. To be honest we weren't *technically* horizontal most of the time now I come to think of it. But that's by the by. Anyway, me bloody leg's still sore where I scratched it, and I've promised your mother I'll get her a new vase to make up for the one I knackered. So I'll have to pop down town and have a look around a few of the charity shops to see what I can find. There's absolutely bugger all else down there these days, apart from coffee shops, fried chicken or burger places, and bookies, and none of them do much in the way of *bric a brac* or *objects d'art*.'

George got up off the armchair he'd been sitting in, and walked over to his son. Then he nudged him on the shoulder.

'But despite breaking your mother's favourite vase she says I've been a good boy for the last couple of days, so we won't be having any whipped cream with our tea because I've got it earmarked for something a lot more interesting.'

'What's that?' asked Leanne, before Brad could tell her not to.

'The pair of you never tried it then?'

'Almost certainly not, but unless you tell us we won't know whether we have or not, will we?'

George smiled and nodded his head in anticipation of being able to regale one of his implausible tales, while Brad shook his in anticipation of having to listen to it.

'One of the lads in my unit tried it when he'd got the undivided attention of a couple of pretty young *frauleins* down in the *Reeperbahn* one night. Some of the things they got up to down there - well, it'd make your hair curl, that it would. Anyway, we were on our way out to the Far East when he told me about it, and it sounded like a bit of fun so I thought I'd see if I could get the luscious Miss Lucy Lee to give it a go when I got out to Malaya. The problem was he kept on telling me about it for the entire bloody journey from east of Suez, so when we eventually arrived in Penang I was off the ship almost before it had docked. Within five minutes I was banging on the door of Mr Patel's Passion Parlour demanding to see young Lucy, or failing her anything without a penis. It wouldn't have been quite so bad if the place had been open at the time, and it might also have been an idea if I'd kept me trousers on, particularly bearing in mind

Mr Patel's place was next door to a busy mini-market on one side and a fishmonger's on the other. I suppose on the plus side it gave me plenty of time to go and buy a pint of whipping cream and a tub of glace cherries, because I hadn't changed my watch since we left Calcutta, and I was taking a chance on them opening up at teatime as it was. Anyhow, after I'd been sat outside for about three hours young Lucy and two of the other girls turned up and let me in.'

'So how did the pair of you get on then?' asked Leanne, despite Brad kicking her on the back of her left leg in a futile attempt to dissuade her from pursuing the subject.

'Not as well as I'd been anticipating unfortunately. Regrettably the delectable Miss Lucy wasn't over keen on letting me use the whipped cream. She'd let me do pretty much anything else mind – and then some, I don't mind telling you..'

'I'd rather you didn't,' protested Brad, but to no avail.

'But on balance the whipped cream wasn't a great success, and she said she wasn't too happy about using glace cherries either.'

'Why not?' asked Leanne, wondering what prevented Malaysian prostitutes from indulging their clients' wishes using preserved fruit, and which sounded perfectly reasonable and potentially quite enjoyable as far as she was concerned.

'Too bloody sweet, that's why,' replied George. 'Too bloody sweet. When I was out there the previous February we'd made the mistake of letting some of that maraschino syrup dribble along dear little Lucy's side-boobs, and the next thing we knew the whole bed was a mass of writhing bodies.'

'That sounds pretty damn good to me,' suggested Leanne, and she squeezed Brad's thigh firmly. 'Maybe we should give it a go? I reckon if that doesn't get things moving down under nothing will.'

'Not like that my dear,' replied George. 'Much the pity I have to say. No, it was bleedin' ants, or termites, or something tropical like that anyway. All over the place they were. Mr Patel got really pissed off because all the girls were complaining they were getting bitten, and so he had to close the passion parlour for a night and have the whole place fumigated.'

'How do you spell that syrup thing Granddad ?' asked Tina who had got up off the carpet and was now sitting cross-legged on a settee opposite George. She was busily scribbling in a large scrap book with a multi-coloured front cover.

'What 'syrup thing' is that darling?' asked Gwen who had just come into the lounge from the kitchen.

'The syrup thing that Granddad said they dribbled under the lady's booby sides.'

'M-A-R-A-S-C-H-E-E-N-O, I think,' replied George. 'I've never really had the need to spell it before. Why do you want to know?'

'We've got an exercise at school doing spelling,' replied Tina. 'We've all been told to find twenty new words we haven't written down before, and then write them how we think they ought to be spelt. Jeffrey's doing it too but he hasn't been told he's got to by his teacher so he's just being a silly copy-cat.'

'Not,' replied Jeffrey, without looking up from his own scrap book.

'Anyhow,' said George, ever eager to broadcast details of the lurid experiences he'd enjoyed during his time in the Senior Service. 'We couldn't use glace cherries on account of those damn termites and luscious young Lucy getting her tits all sticky, so we decided to use rambutans instead.'

'I don't know how to spell that one either Granddad. Can you spell it please?' asked Tina. 'It's not cheating. Really.'

'R-A-M-B-O-O-T-A-N-S probably, but be buggered if I know.'

'Never mind how you spell it, what the hell are they?' demanded Leanne, whose knowledge of tropical fruit left a lot to be desired unless it came out of a tin.

'An exotic tropical fruit native to the Malay peninsula,' replied George. 'Look a bit like hairy plums. You've got to peel them first but they go a treat with whipped cream.'

Leanne grinned and shifted around on the settee so that she could look her husband in the eye. 'Talking of hairy plums,' she said, slowly and suggestively licking her lips. 'How do you fancy having your little rambutans covered in whipped cream sweetheart? I promise not to try and peel them.'

'Behave yourself for heaven's sake woman,' replied Brad, who scowled at the suggestion and unintentionally put his hands across his lap as if to prevent himself being sprayed with pressurised dairy products.

Having suitably humiliated her husband Leanne returned to the subject of George's tropical fruit cocktail and its unorthodox use as a sex aid.

'So what was the problem you and this Lucy Lee woman had with whipped cream then?'

'Heat and humidity,' replied George. 'Heat and humidity. It was bloody hot and humid out in Malaya I'll have you know, and it didn't matter what we did with the whipped cream, we couldn't keep it stiff.'

'Tell me about it,' muttered Leanne, and she looked at Brad out of the corner of her eye as her husband's face turned an intense shade of red. 'I can't even get his little bugger stiff in the first place.'

Fortunately for Brad's blushes George didn't pursue Leanne's revelation of her husband's condition, and instead continued with his own story.

'Anyway, once we'd whipped it up nice and stiff we slapped the cream all over Lucy's lady bits, and shoved on a couple of rambutan halves to top them off. That was easy enough, but trying to keep it all on her once it had warmed up a bit was nigh on impossible. To make matters worse there was a thunderstorm on the way, so the damn cream went all horrible and rancid by the time we got down to the business, and then young Lucy went and got precious about having warm buttermilk running up her arse. We tried it about half a dozen times but she decided enough was enough, and she wasn't having any more of it.'

'Well you would by then, wouldn't you?' said Gwen, who had just returned to the lounge, having popped to the back door to throw a stone at a cat that was busy doing its business on the Dixon's patio. 'I really couldn't be doing with it either. Not buttermilk, oh no, definitely not. Whipped cream, well that's another matter altogether, isn't it George? But buttermilk, oh no. Definitely not for me.'

Brad would have preferred his mother to have been considering the merits of whipped cream when applied between two layers of sponge cake rather than the front side of an oriental prostitute, however his main concern was with the sheer scale of his father's nocturnal leisure activities.

'Bloody hell Father!' he exclaimed. 'Every time we come over here you spin us another of your implausible yarns about that wretched Mr Patel and his bloody Penang Passion Parlour. Do you make them up the day before or are they spontaneous creations?'

'They're all true,' protested George. 'Every single one of them.'

'Well how much time did you spend at that place? I mean, you were supposed to be there serving Queen and Country, not just getting your end away.'

'Oh this particular session was only over a few evenings one June,' replied George. 'It was the height of the wet season, so it was pretty stormy most of the time and we had the same old problems night after night.'

'Tell me about that as well,' muttered Leanne.

'Is that 'R-S-E' Granddad?' asked Tina, waving a blue crayon at George.

'Is what R-S-E sweetheart?'

'Where that lady had the butter and milk. You said young Lucy had butter and milk running up her R-S-E.'

'A-R-S-E,' replied George, much to Brad's annoyance. 'She had buttermilk running up her *arse*.'

'Honestly Father,' snapped Brad, angrily. 'Do you really think this is a suitable conversation to be having with a young lady of Tina's age?'

'She's got to find out about real life sooner or later,' replied George. 'And better sooner than later as far as I'm concerned. It's a tough world out there, and I'd rather that she was streetwise beforehand.'

'I don't really think sordid tales from a Malayan brothel are likely to help a kid in rural Suffolk grow up to be streetwise,' complained Brad. 'I don't actually think any of your stories are really suitable for children. In fact most of them aren't suitable for anyone under, well, for anybody really.'

'What utter tosh and bollocks,' replied George, ignoring his son's protestation. 'So what words have you written down in that book of yours, young lady?'

George took Tina's scrap book, and started running his index finger down a string of words crudely written in capitals and blue crayon.

'That one begins with a C,' he said. 'Not a K. Where did you hear that anyway?'

'At home,' replied Tina. 'Daddy Frank says it when he's watching the television. He says it quite a lot actually, especially when he's been drinking lots of lager or he's watching football. That's L-A-G-E-R, there, look.'

Tina pointed to the word 'Lager' on her scrapbook. It was written under a misspelt but highly offensive noun frequently used as an adjective, and above the word 'nipple' which she had also misspelt 'N-I-P-E-L'.

'He usually says it when that man in a suit stands up and starts talking in front of a lot of other people in suits who are sitting on green seats and waving bits of paper about and being silly and shouting 'arf 'arf 'arf, and then standing up and then sitting down again.'

'She means PMQ,' said Jeffrey, without looking up from his scrap book.

'PMT dear,' replied Gwen. 'You'll find out all about that soon enough Tina sweetheart, don't you worry.'

'No Gran, PMQ – Prime Minister's Questions. That's when Frank says it.'

'The right honourable member my A-R-S-E,' said Tina. 'That's one of the things Daddy Frank says. And another thing he says is 'Never mind all this shite and bollocks about him being an honourable member, as far as I'm concerned he's a right dishonourable C-..'

'Well he shouldn't say that,' interrupted Brad. 'It's not a nice thing to say about anybody, let alone a member of Her Majesty's Government.'

'And he calls that funny man with the blond hair one as well.'

'What funny man is that sweetheart?' asked Gwen.

'The one who wants to be the boss of America. Him. 'How many hundred million people have they got out there?' Daddy Frank says. 'How many hundred million and the best they can find is that C-"

'He shouldn't say that either' snapped Brad before Tina had a chance to finish explaining what 'Daddy Frank' thought about the gentleman concerned.

'So you discovered this thing using cream and exotic tropical fruit by accident did you George?' asked Leanne who was beginning to get bored reading misspelt obscenities from Tina's scrap book, and was curious to find out more about the erotic delights that might be gained from a fresh fruit salad and whipped cream, or possibly even a tin of Carnation for an occasional variation.

'No,' replied George. 'It was something a couple of the lads in my unit said they'd tried out here and there, although I didn't really believe them at the time. I'd become a dab hand spicing things up with a few rambutans or lychees, so the combination of whipped cream and tropical fruit sounded like a match made in heaven. Incidentally pineapple's not bad if you fancy a change from time to time, but you need to make sure it's out of a tin and don't try it with ordinary cream whatever you do otherwise it'll curdle like buggery. I'm drifting off the subject again, aren't I? Now then, what was I saying? Oh yes, when the opportunity to try out a new recipe arose I thought I'd give it a go. Young Lucy Lee said she was up for it if I treated her 'extra special' so I thought 'Why not George me old mate?' I had to shove a few extra Ringgits down her G-string and buy her two glasses of what Mr Patel claimed was 'Champagne' but was clearly nothing of the sort, and tasted like cat's piss, but I reckoned it'd be worthwhile trying it anyway.'

'Bloody hell,' muttered Brad. He sighed and shook his head as George continued with his story.

'Dear old Chalkie White told me he'd tried something similar with a raita and some chicken tikka bits when he was out in Bombay - That's a thing made out of yoghurt and cucumber in case you were wondering. He had to use that because they don't have much in the way of fresh dairy produce out there, on account of a lack of refrigeration and their cows all being scared. Or was it because all their cows are sacred? I'm not sure – it's one or the other, and it doesn't really matter which.'

'He didn't *have* to use anything,' said Brad, who was becoming increasingly irritated at his father's seemingly more bizarre and never ending tales. 'He could have just gone out for a nice meal, or a beer, or, or, or something else. *Anything* else in fact. He didn't *have* to end up in some sleazy back-street knocking shop with a fifty Rupee tart.'

'Oh I don't think he paid as much as that,' replied George. He scratched his nose. 'You could get a brace of them for not much more than thirty five in those days - or maybe forty at a pinch - plus the price of the refreshments.'

'Where did the cucumber come in?' asked Leanne.

'Chopped up in the yoghurt,' replied George. 'Why?'

'I was just wondering, bearing in mind some of the stuff you come out with.'

'Anyway, as I was saying - Chalkie got this raita and some pieces of chicken tikka, and spent what he described as a bloody good session's grazing. Mind you, he didn't half suffer for it afterwards.'

'Why,' asked Leanne. 'What happened?'

'He had a right royal dose of the shits for over a fortnight. Lost two stone he did. Two stone, one of his socks, and his wallet. I can't honestly say I was surprised by any of it. In fact the cotton in his underpants had perished by the time he was back on solids. Now that *did* surprise me.'

'Served him bloody well right,' muttered Brad. 'And it'd serve you bloody well right too.'

'Shits,' said Tina. 'S-H-I-T-Z.'

'S-H-I-T-S,' replied George. 'It's the plural so it's got an S on it, not a Z.'

'So this Chalkie White's experiences in Bombay inspired you to have a go with whipped cream and glace cherries when you got out to Malaya, did it?' asked Leanne, causing Brad to start to wonder if his wife might be developing similar ideas with a view to finding a holistic cure for his condition, and an end to several months intense frustration for herself.

'Not really, no. Me and the lads had started developing a few ideas after sampling some of the exotic delights on offer in Japan. Now, before you say anything Bradley, just let me make it perfectly clear that visiting the sort of fine establishment that Mr Patel used to run on Penang wasn't an option when I was out in Japan.'

'The inscrutable Japanese having far higher moral standards presumably?'

'No, they were too fucking expensive.'

'Language please George,' said Gwen. 'Young ears are listening you know.'

'Sorry dear. Slip of the tongue. You know how it is.'

'I used to,' muttered Leanne, before George continued complaining about the cost of exotic entertainment in Japan.

'Everything that's important is bloody well over-priced in Japan. Food, beer, you name it. You can almost buy a spare tyre for a Ford Mondeo back here for the price of a packet of condoms in Yokohama, and just think how much more rubber there is in a SR900 radial than in an organically lubricated Nippon Extra Length skin. So in view of the extortionate demands that a night's unbridled enjoyment was going to place on our wallets we decided to just go and have a meal, and perhaps see if we couldn't convince a couple of the local girls that they needed to find out how much meat some western men pack in their lunchboxes. But to be honest we didn't hold out much hope, so when me and four of my mates found ourselves with a free weekend in Yokohama we had to find something else to keep ourselves occupied. Now normally we'd have welcomed the opportunity to spend our free nights indulging in some of the more exotic local oriental specialities, but as I've already told you those types of specialised activities are bloody expensive, and frankly for the price of one in Japan you could get at least three in Penang – possibly all together on the same mattress if they weren't over busy at the time - five in Bangkok provided you didn't want a ladyboy included, and a full session in every establishment in an entire bloody street in Mombasa, although frankly even I wouldn't want to risk that one. So although your Japs may be world leaders in engineering and technology they're really piss poor value for money as far as the pleasures of the flesh are concerned. Anyway, that left us wondering what on earth we were going to find to do for a night's entertainment that wasn't going to cost us a small fortune. Fortunately my old mate Stinker

Harris said he knew a bloke called Mr Konishi who ran a place offering what he called '*Nyotaimori*'.'

George paused briefly, allowing Jeffrey time to ask a question.

'Why was he called 'Stinker' Grandad?'

'There are some things in life it's better not to know, and that's one of them, believe me,' replied George before carrying on from where he'd left off.

'I'd never heard of this *Nyotaimori* thing – and don't you go asking me how to spell it young lady because I've absolutely no idea – and it was bloody expensive too, but Stinker assured us it was a 'sensuous celebration of food and fertility' - if not fornication – and it was worth paying a bit extra for.'

'Wouldn't it have been a lot simpler to just have gone and found a kebab shop or something?' asked Leanne.

'Well as things turned out that might have been a better option, but we weren't to know that at the time. But anyway, as I was saying, this Mr Konishi had told Stinker he could do the six of us a cut-price deal. So we thought about it for a couple of minutes and decided to give it a go. It turned out that this Konishi bloke was running his operation from a two-bed flat in a rather grotty back street near the railway station, but as our normal stomping grounds were similarly located it didn't really bother us.'

'So what does this Nyo- thingy actually involve?' asked Leanne who, true to form, was beginning to wonder if it might help alleviate Brad's condition, in which case she thought she'd probably be happy to give it a go, provided it didn't involve unpeeled tropical fruit with which she was unfamiliar, rancid cream or anything too weird.

'Eating a meal off a woman's naked body. Sushi normally I believe. It can also be off a man's body but there's no fucking way..'

'George!'

'Sorry dear. No, there was no way anybody was going to convince me to eat my dinner off some bloke's hairy arse.

'A-R-S-E,' said Tina. 'A-R-S-E spells arse.'

'She's getting the hang of that one, isn't she?' grinned George, before continuing with his explanation of what Brad mistakenly considered a bizarre sexual practice masquerading as an ancient oriental art.

'As far as I was concerned a woman it had to be. And as it turned out Mr Konishi's niece was happy to oblige, even if she was about twenty years his senior, although we didn't know that at the time either because we paid in advance in return for that hefty discount which just about allowed our wallets to stretch to it.'

'You were fucking had,' said Leanne, to which Gwen scowled at her daughter in law and wagged her finger furiously. 'You were had, weren't you George? Admit it.'

'I wish I bloody well had been,' George said and nodded his head. 'Anyway, when we got back to Konishi's place we were all shown into his front room and asked to sit down. But there were no chairs, and so we complained and then Konishi said we'd be sitting on the floor because we were going to eat Japanese-style. That sounded fair enough, and so we waited to see what was going to happen next. Then Konisihi's niece comes into the room dressed in one of those one-piece outfits. You know, the ones that are really difficult to get into or out of? I forget what they're called.'

'You mean a onesie?' suggested Leanne.

George shook his head. 'No, a kimono. That's it. Red and black, and covered with fancy silk embroidery showing the Japanese countryside in the autumn. Very tasteful it was, although I've no idea what a flock of flamingos was doing there, so perhaps it was supposed to be somewhere else altogether. Or perhaps they were swans and not flamingos? They'd got long necks anyway, whatever they were. But I'm digressing again – So as I was saying, this niece of Konishi's – 'Chiharu' he said she was called. I looked the name up later, when I was back in England, and it means 'One Thousand Springs'. Well to be honest I reckon she'd seen about seventy of them herself, but Stinker said we'd got a bargain and after all you pays your money and you takes your choice.'

'You're still digressing,' said Brad. 'Just get on with the rest of the story *if* you absolutely must, and try not to make it too vulgar bearing in mind you've got your grand-son and grand-daughter here with us.'

George looked at Brad and tilted his head to one side. 'Get out of the grumpy side of the bed this morning, did we Bradley?'

'No. The floppy side,' retorted Leanne. 'He's been doing that a lot recently, haven't you dear?'

'Sounds to me like you need to treat yourself to a new mattress my old son,' laughed George. 'Reckon the pair of you have gone and worn the old one out. If the springs have gone it's probably metal fatigue. Mattresses don't last like they used to, do they Gwen? Believe me, I should know.'

'There's nothing wrong with our mattress, thank you,' replied Brad.

'Whatever. Anyway, as I think I was saying before I got interrupted – This niece of Konishi's walks into the centre of the room and then slowly unwraps her kimono – bleedin' yards of it there were – and chucks it into a pile in the corner. So now she's standing there naked and I'm thinking this is quite a promising start. Then she gets herself down on the mat in the centre of the room. It's getting more like Mr Patel's place by the minute, and I'm beginning to wonder if it's all quite what it seems. But then Konishi starts beckoning us to sit down and take our places around his niece, who's laid out flat on the floor - face up - displaying her most tangible assets. So we all sit down around this human warming plate, Stinker at her head and two of us either side, and Konishi starts handing out these bamboo chopsticks. It's only then we realise that we're supposed to pick up tasty morsels off this woman by leaning forward and using these wooden bits of twig. Well, Bomber Harris isn't having any of it and asks why we can't use knives and forks to which Konishi says something about health and safety. We think that's what he said, although we were never quite sure to be honest. But if you think about it, removing food from a naked body with a knife and fork *could* be a bit of an health and safety issue, particularly if you were having steak, so that's probably what he was on about.'

'For heaven's sake just get on with it and be done Father.'

'Alright Mr Grumpy. What's all this about you getting out of the floppy side of the bed then?'

'I don't want to talk about it right now if you don't mind,' replied Brad, his face again turning a vivid shade of red.

'He won't talk to anybody about it apart from Dr Raja, and that's the problem,' said Leanne. 'I wish he bloody well would, because talking to Dr Raja's a total waste of time. I'm not even sure he's a real doctor to be honest, or if he is his Doctorate's in something entirely unrelated to medicine.'

To both Brad's and Leanne's surprise George didn't return to his far-fetched story, but reached out and placed his hand on his son's arm.

'We'll have a bit of chat when you're good and ready Bradley. Don't you worry. We'll see if we can't rub some of my extraordinary virility off on to you.'

'Urrgh,' groaned Jeffrey, and stuck his head into his scrapbook so nobody could see his face or the fact that he was giggling.

'So where was I?' said George, his moment of unexpected compassion seemingly at an end. 'Oh yes. I'd just told you about Bomber not wanting to use chopsticks, hadn't I? Right, well then Bomber says he don't know how to use those chopstick things anyway, and be buggered if he's even going to try what with his back being in the state it is. I didn't know it at the time, but Bomber and Mick 'The Dick' O'Keefe had been having back problems since overdoing it big-time when they were out in Bombay. So with these kinds of cultural differences we were getting a bit worried that we weren't going to be getting any dinner tonight, and so we asked Konishi for our money back.

Needless to say he wasn't having that and started swearing at us and cussing - we assumed that was what he was doing but it was difficult to tell as he was jabbering away in Japanese. But then, just as we thought he was about to pull a Samurai sword on us, the naked niece Miss Chiharu gets up off the floor, turns over and gets into a prone position on her hands and knees. Uncle Konishi grins and waves his hands around, and beckons us to sit down around his niece again as if she's some kind of human table – which was exactly what she was going to become. It was all quite cosy really although Bomber had to shift his left leg to one side a bit because it was rubbing on Miss Chiharu's dangly bits and getting her all unnecessarily distracted. I actually think he was doing it deliberately, and I can't say I blame him. I mean, given the opportunity I'd probably have done the same.'

'He's always been a bit of a one for ladies' dangly bits. Haven't you dear?'

'I have Gwen my dear, that I have. You can't beat rummaging around a nice set of ladies' dangly bits, I always say. I said it down the Pig & Whistle once, but I don't think that miserable cow behind the bar took very kindly to it and they haven't let me in there since.'

'Get on with it Father.'

'Alright, alright. Keep your hair on. Now where was I? Oh, yes. I was telling you about Bomber and how his leg was rubbing was Miss Chiharu up the wrong way, wasn't I? Yes, that was it. Well, once we were all sat down again Konishi brings in a pile of tin foil containers with our dinner in, and proceeds to dish it out onto Miss Chiharu's back. After about five minutes he'd set out the complete meal – a neat pile of sliced raw tuna on her left shoulder, some thinly carved slices of Kobe beef *carpaccio* on her right, an arrangement of salmon *negri* on the upper three vertebrae, and so on. The final item on the night's menu was a light soy dipping sauce which Konishi poured into the small of Miss Chiharu's back once all the food was in place. Really quite artistic it was. Anyway, the banquet was all laid out ready for us to tuck in then in comes Pickled Ginger.'

'I know it's a traditional accompaniment to Japanese food but I can't say I'm particularly keen on pickled ginger,' said Brad, who had managed to remain silent while George had been recounting this part of his unlikely tale because for once his father's recollection of events hadn't been overly revolting, albeit it had been typically explicit. 'It's got a very strong taste and I find it tends to overpower the gentler, more subtle flavours.'

'Not 'pickled ginger' you posh twat,' retorted George. "Pickled Ginger.' That was his name.'

'Who the hell is going to call their son Pickled Ginger?' demanded Brad.

'It was his nickname. His real name was John McFee, but he'd got a shocking mop of ginger hair – and I know it was real because I'd seen him in the showers - and the 'Pickled' bit came from his over consumption of fermented grape juice, or other beverages of the intoxicating variety. Hence 'Pickled Ginger'.'

'You mean he was a piss artist,' said Leanne.

'Exactly. He'd been a bit late turning up on account of needing to pee out his first couple of gallons of the evening, and there didn't seem to be that many public lavvies in Yokohama. So poor old Ginger was faced with having to slash up some side alley and risk being caught, and he wasn't sure the Japs would be that happy if they caught him because from what we'd seen of the place they seemed to differ from us here in the West by not pissing in lifts and phone boxes. I'm really not sure why that is bearing in mind how convenient they are when you can't find a public bog anywhere. It's just a cultural thing I suppose, and no doubt they'll catch up with us sooner or later. Anyway I'm digressing again - The only other option was to try and find a friendly barman who might let him use their facilities. He couldn't just walk in to a bar - all nonchalant, like you'd do here - and use the bog and bugger off again before they realised you hadn't bought a pint, primarily due to him being the only ginger amongst about half a million black-haired Nips. So he found a place that looked like the management might be amenable and tried to ask them if he could use their lavvy. Of course they hadn't got a bloody clue what he was on about, so he tried to mime having a pee instead. Fortunately they understood what he meant, which was just as well because as soon as he'd got inside their bogs he discovered the previous night's *teriyaki* chicken with prune puree had done its work which was hardly surprising considering he'd been diagnosed with IBS only a week before we set sail. So although he was a bit late getting to the meal at least he didn't get banged up for leaving an unwanted calling card in a public place.

'You're digressing again Father,' complained Brad. 'For heaven's sake just tell us about the meal and be done with it. We really don't want to hear any more about your mate's bowel disorders if you don't mind.'

'Alright, alright Bradley. Just be patient will you. You've made me lose me place now. Where was I? Oh yes, I remember - Now the six of us are all sat down we're ready to start tucking in.

Of course, as he turned up last Ginger had to fit in as best he could, and with Stinker sitting at the front end and two of us either side of Miss Chiharu the view Ginger got wasn't quite as appealing as it could have been because there was only one place the poor bugger could dump himself.'

George paused for a few seconds and scratched his crotch. 'Actually, that's not a particularly good choice of words now I come to think of it.'

'I think we all get the picture,' said Brad. 'There's really no need to tell us anything more.'

'Anyhow, we're about to tuck into the food and then Ginger discovers he can't use chopsticks either, and the only way he can get anything up to his mouth is to spear it. Fortunately it seems that Japanese chopsticks are more pointed than the Chinese ones, so it worked a treat and before you can say 'Kamikaze' old Ginger is shovelling away slices of yellow-fin tuna like it's an endangered species which, as I understand it, it may soon well be.'

'K-A-M-I-K-A-R-S-E' said Tina.

'That's almost it,' replied George. 'Kami with a K and an arse.'

'So what went wrong?' asked Leanne. 'Because when you started you said it might have been a better idea to have just gone for a kebab or something.'

'Too right I did. We were all tucking in and having a great old time, especially Mick the Dick who'd got one hand busy adjusting Miss Chiharu's protuberances despite being told not to. Purportedly he was doing it so they didn't rub on his leg, although she didn't see it that way and complained to Konishi who told Stinker to keep his mate Dick under control. I remember what he said to this day, that I do.'

'Which was what?' asked Leanne, just in case George didn't elaborate.

'Now look here Mick, this is fucking art this is, so no touching, alright?'

'I won't tell you again George!' shouted Gwen, before turning her wrath on her daughter in law.

'You're just encouraging him you are, you and your horrible foul mouth. You're vulgar and cheap and common, that's what you are, and you always have been ever since the day my darling Bradley bought you back here. I never really liked many of Bradley's girlfriends, but he once brought a lovely girl back home to meet me. Only the once mind, because the next weekend you turned up with your foul mouth, slutty clothes and nasty habits. Nasty, vulgar, cheap and common, that's what you are.'

'Am I bollocks,' replied Leanne, to which Gwen crossed her arms and turned her back on her daughter in law, allowing George to continue his unlikely tale.

'Well it's good to see you two are getting on so much better these days. Right then, as I was saying - We were all having a great old time until Stinker points to the one remaining king prawn and says, 'Right, who's having that last little bugger then?' and we all look at it. And a most tantalisingly seductive piece of seafood it was too. Now in polite company - such as your mother's - I'm sure we'd all have offered it to another person, but some of my mates weren't really how you might say 'refined in their ways', and all decided they wanted that prawn themselves. The outcome wouldn't have been so bad if Ginger hadn't suddenly lashed out with his single pointed chopstick in the direction of the prawn, and if his aim had been a bit better. As it was he was a bit off target, which was either because of all the beer and the rice wine he'd put away, or because his glasses were all steamed up. Either way, his chopstick ended up where it wasn't intended and Miss Chiharu almost shot through the roof. Needless to say our dinner party was well and truly over, and we sure as hell weren't going to be getting any pudding.'

This part of his tale now having reached a conclusion, George sat back in his chair, smiled from ear to ear, and waited to see how Brad and Leanne would react to hearing about Ginger's grand finale. Surprisingly the first person to speak was neither of the above.

'A-R-S-E' said Tina. 'Arse.'

'Exactly,' replied George. 'The poor woman.'

'No Granddad, I've got twenty words now. Look.'

Tina held up her scrapbook so that her Grandfather could see her newly acquired examples of gross profanity, and began to read them out one at a time, in alphabetical order.

'A-R-S-E. Arse. B-O-L-L-O-X. Bollocks. C-..'

'Let me stop you right there young lady,' interrupted George, before Tina could progress from 'B' to a far more dangerous vowel. 'It's B-O-L-L-O-C-K-S, with a C-K-S, not an X. I know it sounds like it should be an X, but it's the plural again, so it isn't.'

Brad was about to try and stop his father encouraging Tina to spell out any more of her newly acquired vocabulary when he heard the front door slam shut.

'Don't worry Bradley, that'll just be your sister Zara,' announced Gwen, just in case Brad had forgotten her name. 'Right then, now she's here I'll start getting the food out.'

'I'm not sure I'm really that hungry,' replied Brad, mindful of his mother's unorthodox combination of fillings for her teatime sandwiches.

'Nonsense dear, I've made us a lovely spread, although I must admit I'm not feeling particularly hungry myself. Hello darling.' Gwen waved to her daughter as she walked into the lounge, and then ruffled Jeffrey's and Tina's hair. 'Say hello to Mummy, you two.'

'Yeah whatever,' replied Jeffrey grudgingly, while Tina failed to respond at all.

Zara took off her coat and threw it onto the back of an unoccupied chair, and issued the briefest of greetings.

'Hello.'

Brad, Leanne and George muttered various greetings in return as Zara sat herself down cross-legged on the floor next to her daughter.

'Frank not with you today then?' asked Leanne, noting that Zara was alone and sensing an ideal opportunity to pry into her sister in law's private life. 'Everything alright between the two of you I hope?'

'Everything's fine thanks. Frank got called away down to Wales urgently to carry out unspecified Army business.'

'Oh, I see,' replied Leanne. She tapped the side of her nose with her index finger. 'Gagging for it again, was she? This unspecified 'Army business'.'

'Don't talk nonsense,' replied Zara, but Leanne wasn't finished just yet.

'Must be nice that - Having a lusty, hot-blooded military type at your beck and call.' She turned her head to look at Brad. 'Especially one capable of hoisting his military standard at a moment's notice.'

'At your beck and call, my dear,' laughed George. 'At your beck and call. I've never been known to fail to rise to the occasion in my life, although that's obviously not something that runs in the family from what I've heard this afternoon.'

'Just shut up,' snapped Brad, although it wasn't clear whether his anger was directed at his father or his wife. If it was the latter then she wasn't listening.

'What was the name of the last one? Oh yes, I remember - Myfanwy wasn't it? Frank had her name tattooed on his arse, but the tattooist couldn't spell it. I remember you telling us about it.'

'A-R-S-E spells arse,' said Tina. 'I can spell arse.'

'Very good young lady,' said George. 'You've got the hang of that one. Now, try 'bollocks' again. And don't forget it's not spelt with an X.'

'Don't you dare!' demanded Zara. 'What are you doing there anyway?'

Zara grabbed Tina's scrapbook, opened it at a random page and started reading. Then, after she'd read a few lines she slapped her daughter across the top of her head.

'That's for being disgusting,' she said. 'I'll have a word with your grandfather later because I've got no doubt he put you up to this.'

George had no intention of denying responsibility for his granddaughter's profane new vocabulary and decided to stand his ground.

'You leave her alone,' he said. 'I'm teaching the pair of them some of the stuff they're not going to learn at school. They can't afford to go out into the big wide world without knowing how to express themselves properly. I mean, if Jeffrey's going to start coming out with phrases like '*I say you jolly old chaps, it's all rather beezer around here, don't you know*' when he's down the boozer people are going to think he's fucking odd.'

'I don't care,' protested Zara. 'That disgraceful scrapbook's going straight into the dustbin when we get home. I'm not having it in my house. And will you please stop using that kind of foul language in front of my children.'

'I'm not having it in my house either, or for that matter anywhere else,' muttered Leanne, just loud enough for Brad to hear.

'So this Konishi threw you and your mates out, did he?' asked Brad, who was anxious to avoid having Leanne wind him up any further, and also to discourage his father from getting into an argument with Zara.

'Yes, and I can't say I blame him. I mean, he was hardly going to believe Pickled Ginger harpooning poor Miss Chiharu up the starfish with a pointy stick was an accident, was he?'

'I don't want to know, I really don't want to know. Whatever this is about, I really don't want to know,' said Zara, and she got up off the floor ready to go into the kitchen to see if Gwen needed any help with the tea. 'Starfish. That's S-T-A-R-F-I-S-H darling. Although they live underwater they aren't actually fish, and they don't have gills, or scales or fins the way that real fish do. And if Granddad offers to draw a picture of one for you in your scrapbooks you're not to let him. Do you understand?'

'Rotten spoilsport,' muttered George.

With both Gwen and Zara out of the room George decided to raise the subject of Brad's condition, despite Brad having told his father not five minutes earlier that he didn't want to talk about it.

'So, from what I gather Mr Wobbly's not rising to the occasion these days then?'

'I already told you that I don't want to discuss it,' said Brad, and he turned away from his father and folded his arms. Unfortunately George didn't take the hint.

'Don't worry son, you're not alone. One of the lads I knew out in Malaya suffered from it too. He didn't usually come along with us when we went out on the town for obvious reasons, although we took him along the first time, and told him he could watch if he thought it might help.'

'And did it? Help I mean,' asked Leanne with what Brad regarded as unseemly optimism.

'No, not a bit. We didn't know what his problem was when we first met him, and so we took the piss out of him something rotten. But then we learned he'd seen active service fighting those communist guerrillas, and the experience had affected him downstairs. Once we knew that we were more sympathetic to the poor old bugger.'

'So do you mean he'd been traumatised by what he'd seen?' asked Brad.

'No, not by what he'd seen. But traumatised certainly. Apparently he'd been out on patrol in the jungle with a few lads from his Regiment when they came across a group of insurgents. There was an exchange of gunfire and he got his bollocks shot off. It was a bit of a shame it was one of his mates that did it. They call that 'friendly fire' don't they? Friendly fire my arse.'

'A-R-S-E spells arse and B-O-L-L-O-C-K-S spells bollocks,' said Tina. 'I can spell arse and now I can spell bollocks as well. Aren't I a clever girl!'

'Very good,' said George. 'Very good indeed. You *are* a quick learner.'

Tina smiled, however her smile quickly disappeared as Zara returned from the kitchen and smacked her daughter hard across the backs of her legs.

'Right young lady, you're coming home with me right now. Get your coat Jeffrey, and get Tina's as well please. You're not having any tea tonight, and just as soon as we get home you're going straight up to your room. The rest of you will have to get your own tea because Mother isn't feeling very well so I've told her to go and have a bit of a rest. Father – Go and see if she's alright will you? Brad – There's some salad and other stuff in the kitchen – I've absolutely no idea what some of it is, and frankly I'm not sure I want to. So if you want to stay and risk it you can help yourself. Otherwise I'll see you all when I see you.'

With that Zara grabbed her daughter by the arm and marched her off to the hall to collect her coat from her brother, while George, Brad and Leanne remained sat down, in a state of bemusement, in the lounge.

'Well fancy that,' said George as he got up out of his chair to go and see how Gwen was. 'I wonder what that was all about? It was probably a woman thing - penis envy I shouldn't wonder. I mean to say Bradley, yours might not work in the prescribed manner but at least you've got one.'

# Chapter 5

It had taken Louise most of the day to get the Hidden Lake's clubhouse prepared for the evening's Valentine dance. She'd had a couple of helpers, it was true, but she liked to think that the evening's décor was primarily down to her own efforts. And Louise had good reason to want to claim credit for her work, because the clubhouse was now decked out in traditional Valentine's Day colours, with red and black helium-filled balloons tethered by colour co-ordinated streamers, and new red tablecloths covering the club's rather motley collection of tables. Now the clubhouse lights had been dimmed to give the room a romantic ambience for the evening – although they hadn't been dimmed too much because Louise didn't want to give the club's evening guests any suggestion that they'd been invited to some kind of impromptu knocking shop. After all, Louise's friend Anna had worked bloody hard to get the six visitors she'd proudly reported to the club's Executive Committee, so if any of the club's errant members so much as dared to throw their car keys onto the dance floor as some kind of a sick joke there would be hell to pay. Louise would see to that, personally.

With the clubhouse decorated to convey an air of tasteful sophistication rather than gaudy decadence, Louise felt that she'd done all she could to help convince Anna's guests they'd done the right thing by spending Valentine's night at the Hidden Lake Club rather than elsewhere. It was now down to the club's members to make their visitors welcome, and for Vic - the club's resident if slightly vintage DJ - to make the night go with a real swing. There was nothing more Louise could do but.. Oh *shit*, where was the wine? There was supposed to be wine on the tables, and little chocolate hearts covered in red foil. A bottle on each table of red wine and white wine – they don't make black wine after all – but where the hell was it? Still in the damn kitchen, that's where, along with the boxes of chocolate hearts.

Verging on a last minute panic attack Louise went off to the kitchen to retrieve the white wine from the kitchen's large refrigerator, only to find her helpers had decided to store the red wine in there as well. Quite what the club's visitors would make of chilled red wine Louise hated to think, so she took the bottles out of the fridge and shoved them into a large bowl of hot water. It was while Louise was busy heating up the bottles of wine that the evening's guests started to arrive, so it was fortunate that Anna was at hand to welcome her prospective new members, and accommodate them with the club members she felt would be least likely to upset, antagonise or insult them. As far as Anna was concerned Brad and Leanne both fell into that category, so when they arrived to grab themselves prime spots for the evening Anna was quick to let them know they'd be acting as host and hostess for the night.

'I've put one couple with Alison and Steve, the other couple with Terry and me, and the single lady – Zoe her name is if you haven't met her - with you, Gwen and George. I thought it would be rather nice to show her how family-friendly we are here.'

'We're not sitting with his sodding parents for the whole evening,' moaned Leanne. 'In fact I'm not sitting with the pair of them, end of.'

'I'm not actually sure they're coming,' said Brad. 'I just got a strange text message that said something about Mother but I've no idea what.'

'Give me your phone,' snapped Leanne. 'Honestly Brad, you really must learn how to use that damn thing.'

Leanne grabbed Brad's mobile and soon established that Gwen wasn't feeling well, that she and George would not be attending the evening's event, and that George had other activities planned on account of Gwen's incapacity.

'How did you work that out?' Brad asked once Leanne had translated from text speak into real words. Leanne gave her husband his phone back but the letters GWEN FUBB SPANKING MONKEY 2NITE 'SUP YO? still didn't make a lot of sense to him.

'Oh, and he wants to know how we are,' she said. 'So if you text him the letters M-E-H that'll do.'

Brad did as he was told and reconciled himself to never understanding something the average nine year old and even his elderly father apparently took for granted.

*** 

The clubhouse was beginning to fill up with the club's members and the evening visitors, and from the number of people it was clear the event was going to be well attended. Brad and Leanne had just invited a couple of their friends to occupy the places that had been reserved for Gwen and George, and the two couples were just getting themselves organised when Anna introduced their guest for the evening, a tall woman with long blonde hair who was wearing a red, knee-length dress and matching high heeled shoes.

'I've put you over here Zoe - with Brad and Leanne. Brad's parents Gwen and George should have been here too, but unfortunately they couldn't make it.'

'So you'll have to put up with us,' said Leanne's friend Julie, and she let out a slightly forced laugh in an attempt to try and make Zoe feel at home. But Zoe appeared more at home than might have been expected.

'Brad?'

'Zoe?' replied Brad, with an air of surprise in his voice. 'Not Zoe Hopkins?'

'Yes it is. Zoe Hopkins originally, and Zoe Hopkins again at present actually, after three years of being Zoe Hopkins-Wilkinson. My God Brad, it must have been ten years.'

'At least.'

The two-way exchange between Brad and Zoe appeared destined to continue unabated until Leanne decided to spoil the party and make herself known.

'Hi I'm Leanne. Brad's wife.'

'Hello Leanne, I'm pleased to meet you. I'm Zoe. Sorry, I can't *believe* this.'

'Yeah, so I gather. I take it you know Brad?'

'Er, yes. We used to work together for, what, a couple of years? And before that we were at primary school together. He was in the year above me, and I seem to remember I had a bit of a crush on him.'

Brad looked upwards, as if to see if the number of years he and Zoe had worked together would somehow magically appear on the ceiling. Although it may also have had something to do with Zoe's suggestion that he'd been a childhood heartthrob.

'Probably two, maybe three. I didn't know you were, er..'

'Married?'

'No, a naturist. I mean, I didn't know you were married either.'

Zoe pulled a chair out from under the table which made Brad realise that if he were to act the gentleman he really should have done that for her. It also made Leanne realise that Zoe had chosen the seat next to Brad rather than the other one next to her friend Julie which she would have far preferred. Leanne would also have preferred that Zoe hadn't pulled her chair up *quite* so close to Brad's, because it was far closer to his than her own. It also appeared from the way that her dress clung to her body that Zoe wasn't wearing any underwear.

'So tell us about this husband of yours Zoe,' said Leanne, subliminally adopting a defensive position.

Zoe looked down at the tablecloth and started fiddling around with a piece of lace embroidery around its edge.

'You mean my ex-husband. Well, to be honest it was a case of love at first sight. I suppose I was very impetuous. He swept me off my feet and, well, you know how it is.'

'Not really,' replied Leanne. 'I don't. So tell me. How was it?'

'Well, to start with everything was wonderful. He was so good looking, so romantic, so kind, so attentive, so..'

'Red hot in bed?'

Zoe thought she probably blushed at Leanne's suggestion, but thankfully in the low light it wouldn't have shown.

'Er, yes. Well, yes, absolutely he was. Actually that was probably what caused us to split up. I mean, you can't build a relationship just on amazing sex alone, can you? After a while it gets monotonous.'

Monotonous the sex with her ex may have been, but Zoe clearly recognised what she'd given up.

'I can't even count the hours we'd spend making love each night,' she said. 'Time and time again he'd take me all the way to heaven and back. Sometimes two or three times a night. That's an amazing experience for any woman, don't you think Leanne?'

'I wouldn't really know,' replied Leanne. 'The furthest Brad's ever taken me is probably Stowmarket, and then I ended up getting the sodding bus back home because he got all over-excited. I suspect he was thinking about having a look at some building site or other, rather than the task in hand, so to speak.'

Leanne picked up the opened bottle of red wine that Louise had just put down on the table with one hand, and with her other hand covered by the red tablecloth grabbed her husband's crotch tightly.

'Actually you're right Zoe. Sex isn't everything. In fact in our house it's nothing at all, is it dear?'

Brad's face also turned red, but in his case it was Leanne's grip on his testicles that was causing him to glow noticeably.

'So was your husband a naturist?' Leanne asked, while Brad was rendered briefly incapable of communication, and as she finished topping up her wine glass.

'Oh my God no! He'd never have stripped off in public. It was a girlfriend of mine that introduced me to it. Marie – she goes to the Barnsted swim. If you've been there you've probably met her.'

Leanne replied that she didn't think she had met Zoe's friend Marie, but on the other hand she might have done so she really couldn't be sure one way or the other, not that she really gave a toss anyway. The polite conversation appeared to be petering out until Brad regained the ability to speak, but when he did it only served to antagonise Leanne further by drawing attention to Zoe's evening attire.

'I *do* like that dress you're wearing Zoe. It's very, er, *fetching* don't you think Leanne? New is it?'

'Oh, it's just something I picked up in the High Street the other day,' replied Zoe, and she ran her hands over her body as if to emphasise the way the dress fitted her, which was pretty much to perfection as far as Brad was concerned. 'I thought it would do perfectly for tonight, what with the red and black Valentine's theme.'

'Good idea,' replied Brad. 'Good idea. Leanne's wearing black for the same reason, but she's had that old frock for years now, haven't you darling?'

'Far more years than I care to remember,' replied Leanne, trying not to grind her teeth. 'Bright red suits you Zoe, and it really doesn't make you look too much like a tart. Honestly it doesn't. After all, what is it they say? Red shoes, no knickers.'

'Well I wasn't sure what the dress code is here,' Zoe replied, completely impervious to Leanne's gibe. 'So for convenience I thought I'd leave them off in case you've got an optional 'Naked after Nine' policy like they have at Westlands, in which case I can just slip this off over my head. I'm hoping you have because there's nothing I like better than dancing naked. It's so wonderfully liberating, don't you think?'

Brad noted that this was at least one area where Leanne, Zoe and he could agree, although he did point out that one proviso to the club's policy was that slow dancing whilst naked be restricted to one's own partner. Leanne's friend Julie and her partner who's name Leanne could never remember got up to dance or possibly to avoid further embarrassment, leaving the awkward threesome to continue their conversation.

'So what are you doing these days?' Brad asked in an attempt to return the choice of topics to the evening's guest rather than with Leanne.

'Pretty much anything in trousers I reckon, provided their balls have dropped,' muttered Leanne, but fortunately neither Zoe nor Brad could hear her over the music.

Brad tried to raise his voice so that he could be heard.

'I mean, where are you working?'

'Mostly below the waist, above the knees and between the legs sweetheart,' muttered Leanne. 'It's pretty bloody obvious to me.'

'I'm at Coastlands District Council now. Still in the planning department, and doing much the same sort of stuff we did when I was with you. Are you still at Two Valleys?'

Brad replied that he was, and Leanne wondered precisely what sort of stuff Zoe and Brad did when they were both at Two Valleys Council, particularly if it didn't involve planning. Leanne's pondering might well have been brought to an abrupt conclusion had she accepted Zoe's suggestion that the three of them join Julie and the partner whose name she could never remember on the dance floor. As it was Leanne declined on the basis that it wasn't so long since she and Brad had eaten dinner and she didn't want to get indigestion.

'Oh come on you two, it's my favourite song,' said Zoe and she grabbed hold of Brad's hand in an attempt to persuade Leanne into joining the pair of them on the dance floor. But Leanne wasn't to be coerced by anybody, let alone a tart with red shoes and no knickers.

'Sorry Zoe, but I don't want to get wind, and I sure as hell don't want Brad to. And bearing in mind how close you're sitting to him neither do you, believe me.'

Brad, on the other hand, had his own reasons.

'I don't really do dancing Zoe,' he said. 'I just haven't got the right kind of rhythm.'

'You can say that again,' retorted Leanne. 'He just shakes things about for a couple of minutes and that's about all there is to it. That's the story of my life really, although thinking about it he doesn't even do that much these days.'

'Nonsense,' replied Zoe, and she tugged so hard at Brad's arm he feared she might dislocate his shoulder.

'You just move your body to the music. Do what comes naturally, after all it's not a competition or anything. Come on Brad, show me you've got a wild side after all.'

With that Brad reluctantly got up and followed Zoe onto the dance floor, leaving Leanne to sit and contemplate exactly what kind of a threat this woman might pose, and what she might have to do about it.

# Chapter 6

Although most visitors to the Hidden Lake Club would probably agree that the middle of winter was far from the best time to visit, it was just a fortnight after her chance reunification with her former colleague and his wife that Zoe Hopkins - now happily single once again and gainfully employed at Coastlands District Council – found herself back within its wooded grounds. And the reason for that situation was that Hidden Lake, like many other clubs, relied upon its members to carry out the myriad of maintenance tasks that had been neglected during the summer months, and which required attention before the start of the new season at Easter. So on the last Sunday of every month between October and February those of the club's members who could drag themselves out of a warm, cosy bed – be it their own or somebody else's - would put on sturdy work clothes and spend the best part of a day helping out.

Just as in previous winters the outstanding tasks were many and various, and just as in previous winters they would place a particular burden on the club's plumbers, carpenters, and builders whose skills were always in demand. The club's other members were very welcome to lend a hand with whatever jobs they were best suited, provided that they didn't get in the way or seriously injure anybody. So for Brad, as a local Council Planning Officer with a wealth of experience of planning theory and English planning law, the task to which he was considered to be best suited was obviously having a bonfire. This may have had something to do with one of the club's Committee members contriving a connection between politics, planning and law, and the Gunpowder Plot for which one Guido Fawkes ended up falling from a scaffold and breaking his neck, thereby saving him the ignominy of having his genitals removed while he was still alive. In that respect Brad was certainly faring far better than dear old Guido, because although his genitals were currently not all they should have been, at least he still had them firmly attached to the rest of his body.

However his allocated task for this particular Sunday had come about Brad could not have cared less. There was something thoroughly satisfying about piling lengths of fallen branches high into a big old oil drum the club kept at the far end of the woods, chucking in a pile of oil-soaked rags, and then setting fire to the lot. Maybe it was the symbolism of life being recycled from the dead wood back into the soil via the pile of ash that remained after the fuel had been consumed, or maybe it was just that bonfire duty was a far cushier job than helping Leanne clear a particularly stubborn blockage in the septic tank. Who was to say one way or the other? Today, however, Leanne had been spared the task of diving up to her elbows in sewage, and was happily stripping slender young branches of their offshoots in order to make enough withies to weave a fence around part of the petanque courts. The fact that both Brad and Leanne were busy working their way through the same enormous pile of raw material didn't matter in the slightest, because Leanne wanted the young green wood for her work while Brad wanted whatever else remained. So for the first hour of that Sunday morning matrimonial harmony was maintained, and would probably have remained so for the rest of the day had not Zoe Hopkins also made her way to the far end of the woods to help Brad and Leanne, or at least whichever of them might be grateful for her assistance.

Brad had just tossed a large fork load of brambles and hedge clippings onto the bonfire as Zoe approached him along one of the pathways that ran through the club's wooded grounds. For a moment she was hidden from view by the cloud of white smoke produced as Brad's bonfire objected to having damp material thrown onto it, but despite this both she and Brad waved enthusiastically as soon as they saw one another through the haze.

'Uh oh. Tart alert,' Leanne muttered to herself as she realised Zoe was greeting her husband with a long hug and a peck on his cheek.

'I'm glad you could make it today,' Brad said once Zoe had let go of him. 'They're always keen to get as many people as possible to help out with the maintenance, and at least it's a dry day, even if it is a bit cold.'

'Which is probably why you and your good lady wife have got your clothes on,' replied Zoe, in a half-hearted attempt to bond with Leanne.

'No, there are some jobs that.. oh very funny.'

'So are your parents here today Brad?' Zoe asked, changing the subject now that her attempt at humour had fallen flat on its face.

'No, I got a message from my father to say that they wouldn't be coming today. Apparently Mother is still not her usual self.'

'And thank God for that, say I,' replied Leanne.

'Oh, that's a shame. I was really looking forward to meeting them after what Anna told me. After all, it's so nice to see two or even three generations working together for the benefit of the club.'

'I bet she didn't tell you the half of it,' said Leanne, as a branch she had been attempting to pull out from under a pile finally snapped under the strain. 'His mother's as mad as a hatter.'

'She's just a bit eccentric at times. That's all,' replied Brad.

'A bit eccentric my arse. She's completely off the wall, nutty as a fruit cake and mad as a fish, in fact all three rolled into one and then some. You can take your pick.'

'But I'm sure her heart's in the right place,' suggested Zoe.

'I'm sure it is sweetheart, but unfortunately it's still beating.'

Her annoyance at Gwen's cardiac condition now aired, Leanne picked up a six foot length of stout willow, stripped the branches off with her machete and fashioned the end into a sharp point.

'This'd sort out the mad old bat,' she said, stabbing the willow stake into the loose soil of a recently formed molehill, and narrowly avoiding Brad's left foot in the process. 'Once and for bloody all.'

Her spleen well and truly vented, Leanne returned to the more genteel task of pulling branches from the pile and stripping them of vegetation, leaving Zoe to enquire further about Brad's parents.

'So what about your father – George isn't it?'

Brad confirmed his father was indeed called George, but before he could say a few kindly words Leanne provided an alternative point of view, just as she had for Gwen.

'And as for Brad's father - well, honestly - what is there to say? Brad's father is a law unto himself, and has a library of the most implausible yarns you've ever heard. Apparently he also has testicles the size of tennis balls, and an unusual condition affecting part of his anatomy resulting in an unheard of level of sex drive which Brad's mad mother wrongly attributes to her husband's excessive consumption of monkey glands when in his youth.'

'Perhaps it's his thyroid?' suggested Zoe. 'Or perhaps it's his hypothalamus? I once knew somebody who had a problem with his hypothalamus. Really awful it was.'

'No dear, it's not his hypothalamus or his thyroid. The problem George has is with another part of his anatomy altogether. His penis to be precise. I don't know what the medical term for it is, but Hyper-Active Penis Syndrome – that's almost 'happiness' coincidentally – describes it pretty well. Do you know, when he was completing a routine check-up for osteoporosis a while ago he answered the question 'Do you still get as many erections in the morning as you did when you were in your youth?' with the reply 'No, I still just get the one.' The silly sod.'

'He never said anything about that to me,' said Brad with a surprised look on his face.

'No, I don't suppose he did. He probably didn't want to cause any embarrassment.'

'There's no reason why he should be embarrassed. It's perfectly normal for men to get..'

'Exactly, and that's why he didn't want to cause *you* any embarrassment, you stupid prat.'

Eventually sensing that all was not perhaps as well as it could have been between them, Zoe decided to leave Brad and Leanne to get on with their respective tasks, and find herself something productive to do.

'Look, I'll leave the pair of you to carry on doing what you're doing, and go and see if Anna's got anything she'd like me to help with, because..' Zoe spluttered as a cloud of smoke engulfed the area where she and Brad were standing. 'Because I'm not really dressed for working with bonfires.'

Her excuse made, Zoe turned and started walking away from the bonfire and back towards the clubhouse, leaving Brad and Leanne to carry on their bickering unhindered.

'She's had those jeans taken in specially,' said Leanne, pointing to Zoe with the sharpened end of her stripped-willow death-stake. 'They didn't leave the shop like that, no bloody way. She's had tucks put in to emphasise her curves, and make her arse roll about from side to side in order to attract men - You're not listening, are you?'

'What?' replied Brad, who had been watching the gentle rolling of Zoe's hips, and not listening to his wife's condemnation of Zoe's alleged man-attracting tactics.

'I *said*, she's had those jeans taken in specially to make her arse wobble from side to side and attract men, and from where I'm standing it seems to be working - even if the man in question would turn out to be one huge disappointment in one respect, and a very small disappointment in another.'

'I really don't know what you're on about,' replied Brad, as another great plume of smoke from the bonfire engulfed him.

'Of course I don't suppose you'd noticed those rolls of fat up her side, had you? No, just the rolling arse. Just like all men, except of course you aren't like other men at present are you? I expect she'd soon lose interest if she was faced with what I get faced with – in a manner of speaking - every time I try and get you interested.'

'Look Leanne, you don't *have* to do that if you don't like it. I've told you that before now, but you said you quite enjoy it.'

'I *would* enjoy it if it had some effect. It's not a lot of fun having a floppy.. Well let's not go there now, alright? But I'm carting you off to see Doctor Raja whether you like it or not, because it's time we got you sorted out and then, once you're all sorted out, you can jolly well sort me out because my need is no less urgent than yours.'

The bickering regarding Zoe's seductively rolling bottom and Brad's current condition might have continued for some time, but fortunately George turned up shortly after Zoe had left forcing an early end to hostilities. He was wearing a sports jacket, smartly pressed olive green trousers and newly polished brown shoes, all of which appeared far too pristine to suggest that George had come to the club for anything other than his lunch.

'I hope you two are going to have a shower before dinner,' he said. 'Because you both stink of smoke, and I can't have you sitting next to me smelling like that. It'll put me right off me

Toad in the Hole.' He turned to Leanne. 'Actually I was half expecting to find you up to your elbows in shit.'

'That was last month,' replied Leanne. 'And I'll be buggered if I'm doing it again.'

'I take it Mother's not with you?' Brad asked, although he had to raise his voice over the crackling of the bonfire to make himself heard. 'How is she now? And what's wrong with her anyway?'

'Nothing too trivial I hope?' added Leanne, just quietly enough for George to misinterpret heartlessness as compassion. 'Nothing involving anything less than acute cramps, nausea or projectile vomiting, and preferably all three simultaneously.'

'I think it's probably a women's thing from the way she was describing it. She's certainly in quite a bit of discomfort, so we'll try and make her an appointment to see Doctor Raja tomorrow to see what he thinks. She didn't want any dinner so I've come down here on my own. Right, I'll wander down to the clubhouse now to make sure I get a decent helping.'

With George convinced that dinner was imminent both Brad and Leanne also decided to stop work, lay down tools and get ready to go and get washed.

'I just ran into that old 'workmate' of yours Bradley,' George said just as soon as Leanne was out of earshot. 'You know, the one with the lovely wiggly backside. Zoe something or other she said her name was. I reckon she could get your bedroom furniture nice and firm, even if Leanne can't.'

# Chapter 7

It shouldn't have taken Zoe long to find her way out of the woods and get back to the clubhouse. With a six foot, barbed-wire topped fence around the club's grounds to deter voyeurs all she had to do was choose to start walking in one of two directions, keeping the fence on one side. If it turned out that she'd made the wrong decision and arrived at the lake where the club's log cabin was stationed all Zoe would have to do would be to turn around and walk in the opposite direction and eventually she'd arrive back at the car park. As it turned out Zoe had chosen the wrong direction, and had found herself on the edge of the lake standing at the very spot where Gwen had decided she wanted her ashes scattered. That also meant that Zoe had seen the club's log cabin at the edge of lake, and had admired the scenic views over its waters and across the club's wooded grounds. Unfortunately it also meant that Zoe was about as far away from the clubhouse as she could possibly get, so it was fortunate for Zoe that Derek was just completing a six-monthly safety check of the log cabin's gas heater when she arrived, and that he immediately realised her situation.

'Lost?'

Zoe nodded.

'Right, I'm just finished here so we can walk back to the clubhouse together. Have you arranged to have lunch with us today?'

Zoe had. While some of the club's members were busy attending to maintenance issues, a small group comprising just those who could be trusted to work with food without actually poisoning anybody would prepare a two-course luncheon to be served in the clubhouse at two o'clock. Although some of the club's members – Gwen in particular - regularly complained that two o'clock in the afternoon was really no time to start serving lunch, those responsible for organising the day's maintenance activities were firmly of the opinion that serving it at one o'clock would deprive the club of approximately fifty per cent of its man-hours, bearing in mind that the majority of its volunteers felt the need for a cup of tea and a good natter upon arrival, and didn't actually start doing anything productive until well after eleven.

'I'm looking forward to it,' replied Zoe.

'Well, don't get your hopes up too much. What are you having anyway?'

'Actually I'm not entirely sure. I was talking to an elderly man on the way over to see if I could help Brad with his bonfire, and he asked me if I fancied a Toad au vin or a Coq in the Hole?'

'That'd be George then,' replied Derek. 'He's Brad's father.'

'I told him I liked Coq au Vin if that's what he meant, and he said something like 'Yes it could be good fun provided you didn't get caught, but you needed to make sure there was plenty of ventilation, otherwise it'd rust the thing from the inside just like his mate's had.' Does that make any sense to you?'

'Not really, but it's probably more intriguing than what's actually on this lunchtime's menu. Had George got an elderly lady with him?'

'No, why?'

'It's just that we haven't seen Gwen – that Brad's mother – for a while, and we just want to make sure she's alright. Gwen and George weren't at the Valentine's dance either. By the way, how did you enjoy the evening? I saw you dancing with Brad, and you both seemed to be having a good time.'

Zoe smiled and made a 'horn' gesture with the index and little fingers of both hands to signify her approval. This confused Derek, because he'd used exactly the same gesture in a bar in Ibiza two years ago, and been unceremoniously thrown out into the street by the owner whose wife he'd just apparently accused of sleeping around.

'It rocked!' Zoe said, unwisely attempting to suggest she was a few years younger than she actually was. 'I had a brilliant time. Everybody was really friendly, and of course it helped knowing Brad. I mean, I know some of your other members from the Barnsted swim, but I've known Brad from way back so seeing him again was great.'

'Yes, Anna did say she thought the pair of you were once an item.'

'Oh my God no! It was nothing like that. We just worked in the same office for a couple of years, that's all. There was nothing else going on. I wonder how she got that idea?'

Derek knew full well how Anna had got the idea that Brad and Zoe had once had something going on. In fact it was exactly how the thought had occurred to him, namely by the position of Zoe's hands on Brad's buttocks, and by the way she'd been running her hands over his back when they'd been dancing together on Valentine's night. It was probably just as well that one of the evening's other guests had been busy attempting to chat up Leanne while Brad was otherwise occupied, because if she'd seen exactly where Zoe had been putting her hands there would have been hell to pay, despite the fact that both Brad and Zoe had been fully compliant with the club's close-dancing policies by having their clothes on at the time.

'So what did you and Brad get up to together?' asked Derek, his mind still occupied with the notion that Zoe had at some point got Brad in a condition that poor old Leanne was now unable to achieve. 'I mean - What did you do together when you were at work?'

'I take it you mean what were Brad and I employed to do during the period of time we were working together?'

'Er, yes.'

'Well, if you must know we were both Planning Officers. I actually try and avoid telling people what I do for a living, because they either a) want to object to an application near them and think that moaning to me is the best way to do it, b) they want professional advice and don't want to pay for it, c) they want to moan about gypsies and travellers, or d) they just want to moan about the planning system generally. So that's how I got to know Brad professionally. We were working in different teams most of the time, so we weren't usually working together. But then I got offered a more senior job at another Council and we lost contact. You know the way it is.'

Reluctantly accepting that Zoe's relationship with Brad was probably nothing more interesting than a rekindled friendship, Derek decided it wouldn't hurt to bolster Brad's currency a little.

'Brad's really helped us out with our planning needs over the years. In fact, he got us planning permission to rebuild our clubhouse when it got almost destroyed in a storm a couple of winters ago. Funnily enough, he also managed to get us permission to put that log cabin down by the lake. We didn't actually ask him to, but somehow when the Council issued us with planning permission it had got the log cabin included on it as well. All we'd wanted to do was store a couple of touring caravans round the back of the shower block.'

Derek's summary of Brad's achievements was not untrue, but unfortunately it was incomplete and it didn't take Zoe long to detect a potential anomaly.

'I was just wondering Derek - Does the club come under Two Valleys District Council.'

Derek nodded.

'That's why it was so handy having Brad as a member. He even came down here when the members of their Planning Committee made a site visit, and gave them a guided tour round the club's grounds and facilities.'

The more Derek explained about Brad's involvement in the club's planning application the further he risked dropping him into a quagmire involving his professional protocol and the Council's Code of Conduct. The fact of the matter was, quite simply, that Brad had taken all necessary steps to distance himself from the club's application for Planning Permission. In fact he'd made it quite clear from the outset that not only could he not *deal* with the club's planning application himself, he could not be *seen* to be involved with it in any way, shape or form. So, instead of putting himself at risk of being implicated in any wrong-doing, Brad had nominated a third party to deal with the application on the club's behalf. That person - perhaps unfortunately now that Zoe was back in Brad's social circle - was Leanne. Be that as it may, the major blunder on the Planning Permission that Brad's Head of Department eventually authorised was due to both his Manager and the members of the Council's Planning Committee being distracted by the sight of naked men and women playing miniten together. Brad had seen the draft Planning Permission before it left the office - and had noticed a huge blunder in the way it was worded - but as he could have nothing whatsoever to do with it, Brad correctly decided not to mention the matter to anybody. The fact that the error on the Planning Permission was hugely to the Hidden Lake Club's benefit had absolutely nothing to do with that decision, naturally.

'So Brad handled the club's application himself?' Zoe asked, curious to find out quite how much involvement her former colleague had in the processing, and how much he may have compromised his professional integrity. Fortunately Derek realised the nature of Zoe's questioning and just about managed to save himself from dropping Brad in the sticky stuff.

'Oh no, he'd made it quite clear that he couldn't get involved, so he got Leanne to deal with the application. Once it had been approved he explained that the Council had screwed up and that we'd actually got a lot more than we applied for.'

'You mean the new clubhouse and the log cabin?'

'I think so. It was all very confusing. We applied to rebuild our clubhouse and to store four of our members' old touring caravans around the back of the shower block. So Brad, sorry - Leanne – told us we might as well include those on our application because apparently they also needed permission. Now – and this is where it gets confusing – when our Planning Permission was issued it was for the new clubhouse and for four caravans. Are you with me so far?'

Zoe said she was.

'Now according to Brad the log cabin we let out for holiday accommodation – the one you saw - is *technically* a caravan, because it can be moved from place to place even though it doesn't have to be. That really confused us, I can tell you. I mean, is that actually true? Is our log cabin actually a caravan?'

Fortunately both Brad and Zoe were familiar with one of the peculiarities of English planning law, namely that a log cabin or any other structure designed for human habitation, not exceeding certain dimensions, and capable of being transported from place to place in not more than two pieces - may *legally* fall under the definition of a 'Caravan'. The fact that Brad and Zoe were of one mind on the subject was of itself notable, because in planning circles getting two planners to agree on anything was pretty uncommon, and even getting a majority decision when three were involved was damn near impossible. Another factor that remained nigh-on impossible was getting Brad – or indeed any other planner – to commit him or herself. Zoe was no different.

'Having recently seen your log cabin but not having carried out a detailed inspection, I would say, in my professional opinion and strictly without prejudice, that it probably would, under English planning law, be considered a caravan.'

'Does that mean yes or no?'

'It means I think it is. Probably yes, but maybe no. Look Derek, don't worry too much about that because you'll end up pulling your hair out. You said the club got permission for four caravans, didn't you?'

'We did, yes.'

'So where are the others?'

'We've only got the one,' replied Derek. 'The club's funds wouldn't stretch to any more although we almost.. - Look, it's a long story, it's almost time for lunch and I'm getting hungry. We can talk about it later if you like. So, do you fancy Coq in the Hole, or a Toad in the Van?'

# Chapter 8

It was barely a five minute walk back to the clubhouse back from the log cabin, although if Zoe had managed to find her way by keeping the boundary fence to one side it would have taken her almost twice as long. By the time she and Derek arrived back at the clubhouse and had washed their hands ready to eat most of the other workers had already collected their meals, and taken their places at the six large tables set out for the occasion. Once inside the clubhouse Zoe collected a plate of Coq au Vin from a small serving hatch in front of the kitchen, and looked around for somewhere to sit. She noticed that there was room for one more at the table where Brad and Leanne were sitting, but also that the seats either side of Brad were occupied by the elderly gentleman she'd seen earlier - who she now knew was Brad's father George - and by Leanne respectively, an arrangement which was not entirely co-incidental. The space where another seat could be squeezed in was between George and an elderly lady with blue hair, and just as soon as George had noticed Zoe standing by the doorway looking for somewhere to sit he beckoned her to come and sit next to him. In fact George was just in the process of suggesting to the elderly lady with blue hair that she should 'shift her arse up a bit' so that Zoe's could be accommodated, when Derek took Zoe by the arm and guided her to a seat next to him.

'You're probably better sitting over here today Zoe. George is a dear old soul, but he can be a bit of a one for the ladies, and Gwen's not here to keep him under control.'

'I'm sure he's fine,' Zoe replied. 'He's with Brad so I'm sure he'll behave himself.'

'Maybe, but it's probably not a risk worth taking. Anyway, you wanted to hear about the three other caravans.'

Zoe had wanted to, but she'd much rather have spent an hour or so flirting with George or Brad, or better still with both George and Brad, even if it did involve winding Leanne up.

'So what happened to those other three caravans then?'

'We pulled out of the deal for the other three. I'd made an executive decision, but the rest of the Committee started asking me some really difficult questions such as 'How much money have we got in the bank?' and 'Can we afford it?' and stuff like that. It's a hard job being the club's Treasurer I'll have you know, and for some reason the rest of the Committee thought I ought to know the answers to those kinds of questions. Anyway, the bottom line – which is a technical term we use in financial circles – is that we couldn't afford it, and it would probably have bankrupted the club if we'd gone ahead. Maybe in a couple of years we'll be in a better position and we'll be able to afford them then.'

Zoe agreed that under the circumstances – whatever they were - it was probably better to act prudently. But one thing puzzled her.

'Wouldn't any of the club's members be interested in taking the other three caravans?'

'What, you mean get our members to pay for them, and then rent them out for holiday use? Well I suppose it might be possible, but to be honest we hadn't thought of that. Would they be allowed to? After all, that Planning Permission belongs to the club.'

Derek was correct, the Planning Permission had been issued to the club, but as Zoe suspected it was for the benefit of the *land*. However, irrespective of who was allowed to put caravans on the club's land there was something else bothering Zoe, and the only way she was going to get to the bottom of that it was to have a look at the Planning Permission itself.

'We can have a look at it together in the Chairman's office after lunch,' Derek replied when Zoe suggested she'd like to see the club's Planning Permission. Naturally, had that conversation not taken place at a naturist club there would surely have been an additional comment along the lines of 'And we'll have a look at the Planning Permission too.' As it was neither Derek nor Zoe found it necessary or appropriate to engage in any innuendo on this particular occasion. With the afternoon's immediate business taken care of Zoe made a general observation on what she'd seen of the Hidden Lake Club's grounds that morning, and received a response that she could have interpreted in more ways than one.

'It's a lovely site Derek.'

'That's what I kept telling my ex-wife.'

'Er, yes. I actually meant the club's grounds. The woods are lovely and the view over the lake from the log cabin is gorgeous.'

'The trees are all protected you know. There's a Preservation Order on every one of them. We can't so much as prune the damn things without the Council's say-so.'

Zoe laughed. 'That's what they tell you. Brad knows all about the Council and its Tree Preservation Orders. It was quite a few years ago, but Brad had this application from some guy who wanted to build a house on a piece of land which was covered with mature trees. Oak, Ash, Beech – you name it, it was growing there. So when the guy asks Brad what he thinks Brad goes and tells him he hasn't got any problems with the *principle* of a house on the land, but he wants the Council's Tree Officer to have a look at the trees. The bloke who wants to build the house asks Brad what's wrong with the trees, to which Brad – bless him, the poor lamb – replies there's nothing's wrong with the trees. So Brad gets in touch with the Tree Officer, and tells him that he thinks the trees might be worthy of being protected. Naturally Brad hasn't let the punter know of his concerns, so the Tree Officer goes off and has a look at the site, and agrees with Brad that the trees are – what were his words? - I know, of 'amenity value' so they ought to be protected. The Tree man goes off and does all the paperwork and gets a Preservation Order raised, and then goes off to find two of the Council's politicians who are authorised to sign the Order. He manages to find one, but the others who can sign the paperwork are all tied up in committee meetings, or party meetings, or some other meetings and aren't available. Eventually they manage to get an authorised second signature and the Tree Officer goes off to find the bloke who wants to build the house, and tries to serve the Tree Preservation Order on him.'

'And?'

'He'd already cut all the trees down.'

'So are you saying we can cut our trees down then?'

'No, I'm just saying the bloke who wanted to build the house outsmarted both Brad and the Council, which frankly isn't that difficult if you know what you're doing. If you've already got a Preservation Order on the trees here at Hidden Lake then it's a different matter altogether.' Zoe smiled and then leant towards Derek and whispered. 'But there are ways around it of course, again if you know what you are doing.'

'Which I'm assuming you do?'

'I would like to think so Derek, I would like to think so. Now then, I think there was something you wanted me to have a look at, wasn't there?

'Indeed there was Zoe, indeed there was. But shall we have a look at that Planning Permission first?'

\*\*\*

Zoe followed Derek into the Chairman's office, and at his request sat herself down in a wicker chair next to a window overlooking the club's car park. Derek opened the top drawer of an old metal filing cabinet and retrieved an A4 sized manila envelope, from which he extracted two sheets of white paper, the first of which had the words 'Planning Permission' printed across the top.

'There you are Zoe,' said Derek, as he handed the document to Zoe. 'See what you make of that.'

Zoe took the papers and started to read them. It didn't take her long to give both pages a quick run through, but once she'd read them Zoe started from the very top of the first page and ran through both sheets again, this time line by line, and word by word.

'So you applied to rebuild the clubhouse and to store four touring caravans behind the shower block.'

'You got it in one,' replied Derek, to which he was tempted to add 'Beauty and brains. That's a dangerous combination if ever there was one.'

'Well, what you've got here allowed you to rebuild the clubhouse, and also to station four caravans anywhere within the club's grounds.'

Derek nodded his head. 'That's exactly what Brad told us, but he said there was more to it than that.'

'Yes, he was right. There is.' Zoe put her chin in her hand as if to appear pensive. 'There's actually no restriction limiting the number of caravans the club can have. That may sound crazy, because the Planning Permission says 'Four Caravans' in the description.'

Derek could have been forgiven for wondering if Zoe and Brad were kindred spirits, because they'd actually come to the same conclusion – an almost unheard of occurrence in the planning profession. In fact that conclusion was due to nothing more than Brad and Zoe both being aware of the implications of a celebrated legal ruling, the effect of which was that where a Planning Permission fails to *explicitly* restrict the number of caravans that may be stationed on a piece land, then the description of that Planning Permission alone does not provide any control.

'Brad tried to explain all this, but to be honest he confused the hell out of the entire Committee.'

'I bet he did,' replied Zoe. 'So let me try. What's the difference between four caravans and five caravans?'

'One caravan.'

'And between four caravans and six caravans?'

'Two caravans. Look, where is this getting us Zoe?'

But Zoe wasn't to be hurried in her explanation of the difference between four, five and six caravans.

'Good, so you can count. I feel that's always a useful attribute in a Treasurer. Right then Derek, let's try again shall we? What's the material difference between four caravans and five caravans?'

'I already told you - One caravan.'

'And between four caravans and six caravans?'

'Two bloody caravans. The same as if was the last time you asked me.'

Of course, it wasn't the same as the previous time Zoe had asked the questions, because she'd altered them slightly.

'That's what I thought you'd say, but unfortunately that's incorrect. And unsurprisingly that's where the Council got it wrong too. I didn't ask what the difference was between four and five caravans, I asked what the *material* difference was.'

From the look on Derek's face it was quite clear that he had absolutely no idea whatsoever what Zoe was talking about, and that was because she was speaking in a legalese pseudo-babble that Council planners use when they are unable to communicate in plain English, or wish to baffle people with gobbledegook for one reason or another.

'Okay, let me try explaining it another way. What's the difference between a caravan site with one hundred caravans on, range from twenty to almost ninety years of age can all sit down to lunch together, or attend social events as a group of friends. And do you know something else Derek? Stripped of our designer suits, our Italian shoes, and our Gucci handbags – and I'm talking mostly about our female members on that last item – we are all the same. Naked we are all equal, and nobody can tell that you are an Investment Fund Manager..'

'An ex-Investment Fund Manager.'

'Sorry Derek, I forgot about that. Nobody can tell that you were an Investment Fund Manager until your bank went tits up, that I am a mere Town Planner, or that Anna spends her working hours washing poo and puke off some of the most frail and vulnerable members of society, for which she earns less in a month than you used to take – I decline to use the word 'earn' - in an hour.'

'No Brad, they can't tell - Well, not unless they look in the car park and see that I'm still driving a Porsche 911, that you're driving a shagged-out Fiat Punto, and that Anna has to get a bus, that is. But that's not the point, is it? The point is that I asked you why you didn't tell the Committee that our Planning Permission allows us to use those log cabins as permanent homes. So why didn't you?'

Brad paused briefly before answering. The truth was that he recognised the likelihood of one hell of a bun fight between the club's members once they became aware of the potential for a fortunate few to acquire themselves a holiday home or even a permanent home in the club's delightful grounds. Better in the interests of all concerned, surely, to use the principles of equality and altruism to which he had already alluded.

'I didn't say anything because I didn't want the way the club works to change. What's more I still don't. What I just said about equality was all true Derek. Our members should all be equal, and those less fortunate than others should not be disadvantaged. I'm quite sure you could afford one of those log cabins, and probably the whole bloody lot without too much hardship. Leanne and I would probably be able to afford one if we scraped around in our piggy bank. But I know that Anna wouldn't despite being one of the most deserving people I can think of, and nor would many of our other friends here. So now you tell *me* Derek - Why should those who have the most money benefit at the expense of others? And why should those same people be able to spoil the glorious, natural surroundings we have here by shoving a damn holiday home on them?'

Brad could feel his heart thumping and realised that he'd become red in the face, although bearing in mind how close he'd been standing to the bonfire Derek wouldn't necessarily have associated Brad's rosy cheeks with his annoyance that Zoe had dropped him in the crap, and not for the first time as he recalled.

'That's just the way life is I'm afraid Brad,' Derek replied. 'It's not fair, I agree, but shit happens as they say. It's the way it always has been, and whether you like it or not I suspect it's the way it'll always be.'

Brad shook his head. 'So what happens now?'

'I'm not sure to be honest. The Committee will have to discuss the situation now that Zoe has explained it fully, but I think they'll probably want to rent out sites for five more log cabins to get some extra income. As to exactly who gets to put log cabins on those sites, well that's anybody's guess, but I suspect they'll be offered to the 'Gold' members first. So that already puts you and me at an advantage Brad, whether you like it or not.'

It wasn't anybody's guess as far as Brad was concerned. Gold members might get first call on the sites, but even if they did Brad hated to think of the shenanigans that would go on to make sure those with the most power and money got what they wanted. As Brad pondered the situation Derek gave Brad a conciliatory pat on the shoulder as if to say: 'You tried to shaft us but we found you out. We forgive you, but don't you dare try it again - because if you do it won't be tennis balls bouncing up and down on the miniten courts.'

Having made quite sure that Brad had got the message Derek gave Brad another pat on the shoulder and then started walking back to the clubhouse. Shortly after Derek had disappeared from sight Brad noticed Leanne approaching, and as she got closer he could hear her trying to tell him something he really didn't want to hear. Despite the fact that he hadn't heard Leanne telling him that Zoe had put tucks in her jeans to make her bum wiggle when she first mentioned it, try as he might he couldn't avoid hearing her now.

'I've just heard that there's going to be another five log cabins put up down by the lake. So short of sleeping with the entire Committee – and there's bugger-all point expecting to be able to rent out your services as a gigolo these days - I don't care what I have to do to get us one.'

# Chapter 10

Brad would have forgotten all about his appointment to see Doctor Raja if Leanne hadn't reminded him. After all, he hadn't made the appointment himself and didn't actually want to see Doctor Raja again anyway, bearing in mind how little good it had done him the last time.

'You will soon be doing the sex thing again and all tickety-boo,' Doctor Raja had previously assured him before adding his customary 'Isn't it?' which Brad couldn't be sure wasn't a sign of his physician's uncertainty regarding the prognosis.

Of course the 'sex thing' hadn't been all tickety-boo despite Dr Raja's reassurance, and in fact it hadn't been tickety-anything to the extent that Brad had begun to wonder if there was even a pulse left in the necessary rather-less-than-firmware. But despite Brad's concerns, Dr Raja again concluded that there was nothing wrong with Brad's equipment that some rest and relaxation wouldn't cure.

'Well, can't you damn well give him something for it?' Leanne enquired, rather forcefully. 'I've tried everything I know to get things moving, and the only thing that's getting stiff is my right arm. Surely if everything's in order down there all he needs is a couple of packets of little blue pills? So, if you'll just write out a prescription we'll be done and you can see your next patient. I know the charge for NHS prescriptions is nearly £9 per item these days, but if it fixes him it'll work out at only just over £2.25 per inch, and you really can't complain about that.'

Unfortunately for Leanne Doctor Raja wasn't convinced that medication was the answer, just as he hadn't been when Brad had previously made the same suggestion. Brad hadn't been keen on Leanne accompanying him during his appointment with Doctor Raja – and certainly not during the physical examination when Doctor Raja had pushed and pulled, and stretched and squeezed parts of Brad with which no other adult male had ever made physical contact. Doctor Raja's eventual conclusion, issued when Brad was gingerly tucking things back inside his boxer shorts, did at least concur with his previous assessment - namely that there was nothing physically wrong.

'Physically your gentleman's bits and pieces are one hundred per cent Hunky Dory, Mr Dixon. So I am thinking that your problem is essentially of the psychosomatic variety, isn't it.'

'The psycho-what variety?' replied Brad.

'Psychosomatic. The problem is all in your head. The problem is because you are thinking about it too much.'

'That's all he bloody well can do about it – Think,' added Leanne who was clearly less than impressed with Doctor Raja's response to her personal mid-life crisis, and before Brad could say a word. 'I don't need him *thinking* about it – I need him *doing* it. And preferably with me rather than that Zoe tart with the rolling arse, flabby sides and no knickers.'

'Perhaps that is the problem Mrs Dixon. Maybe at some point when called upon to perform his husbandly duties he was not able to stir his loins sufficiently – maybe he was just too tired – and this event stuck in his mind, isn't it? So the next time you are wanting to arouse his desires, his mind is pre-occupied with worry that he will not be able to get it erecting in the correct and proper manner. Of course, your husband is not knowing that his mind is worrying about it and so, when you are wanting to be enflaming him in your desired manner with your hand or maybe your..'

'Er, let's keep it at that shall we,' interrupted Brad. 'I get the picture.'

'What I am saying, Mrs Dixon, is that your husband needs to clear his mind of the negative thoughts and..' At this point, and for reasons known only to himself, Dr Raja threw his hands in the air. 'It will start popping up again all willy-nilly and ship-shape, isn't it.'

Unfortunately, Leanne remained unconvinced that a clearance of negative thoughts from Brad's mind would do much for what she regarded as virtually a nil willy, and wasn't about to be fobbed off.

'I don't want it bloody ship-shape,' she said, trying hard not to shout lest she be heard in the waiting room which was only a few yards away. 'I want it big and stiff and cock shaped, and as far as I can see it the only way we're going to get it that state is with medication.'

'But this is what I am telling you Mrs Dixon. We are not going to get it that condition with medicine because the problem is all with his head, not his tickety boo ship shape willy nilly.'

'We?' said Brad, who was becoming irritated at being the subject of the discussion, but so far excluded from it. 'We? This isn't some kind of corporate team building exercise you know. What I need is for you, Doctor Raja, to get my bits back in working order by the quickest and least painful means available.

Now are you absolutely sure there's nothing physically wrong? I mean, what about my hormones – are they alright?'

Doctor Raja scratched his head, then put his hand to his chin and briefly looked pensive.

'That is a good point Mr Bradley Dixon. Maybe I did not think of that so, yes, I can do a blood test for analysis, and to do that I will just need to give you a small prick.'

'Don't you bloody dare,' replied Leanne. 'He's already got one. That's what we're here about in case you hadn't realised.'

'With a needle I mean, isn't it. I need to give you a small prick with a needle.'

'I'd much rather you gave him a big prick with some small blue pills if you don't mind.'

Doctor Raja ignored Leanne's suggestion and walked over to a set of drawers where he opened the top one.

'I can do the blood test now for you, but as I have told you Mrs Bradley, I cannot provide medication for your Mr Bradley husband in this case. What is more, excessive use of the medication will lead to it becoming less effective for other patients. Eventually the time will come when popping down these pills will not be efficacious for popping up the affected member.'

'I thought that was when bacteria were evolving resistance to antibiotics?' asked Brad, as he rolled up his sleeve ready for Doctor Raja to take his blood.

'You could be right Mr Dixon Bradley. But it is not worth taking a chance, isn't it?'

'So why can't you give him some then?' demanded Leanne. 'Just in case it does work, in which case the problem would be solved.' Leanne lowered her voice so that only Brad could hear her. 'And if they don't work I'm damn sure I could find some other stud muffin who could make good use of them.'

Despite Leanne's continued insistence Doctor Raja found yet another reason why Brad should not receive the much sought after little blue pills.

'If I am being perfectly honest with you Mr Dixon Bradley and your Mrs Bradley wife it is very much a case of supply and demand. So many people are demanding them these days and there is not the supply. Maybe I get a delivery of a box to the surgery one day and before you know it they are all gone. Like hot cakes, isn't it?'

'More like hot cocks I'd say' muttered Leanne, but Brad had come to another conclusion.

'So what you're really saying is that you've run out?'

'Personally Mr Bradley, no I have not run out. It is the National Health Service that has run out, and it has also run out money. So, for now blood test will have to do, isn't it?'

Doctor Raja took a sealed package containing a syringe and a needle out of the drawer. Then he put an elasticated strap around Brad's arm ready to try and find a vein.

'The blood test will be checking for your hormones Mr Bradley, but I am thinking it is not a genetic condition you are having. That is to say not one you have inherited from your father. He is the most extraordinarily virile man for his age, isn't it? Quite remarkable in fact.'

It took Brad a few moments to realise the implications of what Doctor Raja had just said.

'That's just my luck I suppose. I just wish I'd.. Just a minute - How do you know about my father? More to the point how do you know about his sex drive unless he told you?'

'I had a consultation with your mother yesterday about her condition and the topic arose, so to speak. I am able to say that your father's extraordinary urges are having to remain unsatisfied at the present, but other than that I cannot comment about your mother's illness due to issues of patient confidentiality.'

'I'm not even sure you should be commenting on my father's condition,' replied Brad.

'He is not my patient Mr Bradley, and it is not a medical condition although in a person of his age excessive demands on the cardio-vascular system could lead to increased risk of a stroke.'

'Stroke my arse,' snorted Leanne 'His mother doesn't need to stroke it. From what his father's forever going on about the damn thing keeps popping up all by itself. And that's a stroke of bloody good luck, I'd say. Wouldn't you?'

Doctor Raja didn't reply but managed to find a vein in Brad's arm and took a phial full of Brad's blood to be sent off for analysis. Then he stuck two strips of sticky plaster over a piece of cotton wool, and told Brad to pull down his shirt sleeve. The consultation was over, but both Brad and Leanne were in little doubt that they were no closer to permanently getting the small matter of a permanently small member resolved.

# Chapter 11

Brad had meant to give Gwen a call that evening to find out how she was, but by the time he and Leanne had got home from their appointment with Doctor Raja, and Leanne had decided to get Brad relaxed enough to allow her another attempt at enflaming him using a couple of methods Doctor Raja had suggested it was far too late. Cursing herself for over-reliance on alcohol as a means of inducing relaxation, Leanne pulled the duvet cover over her naked husband, got out of bed, got dressed and left Brad to sleep it off. Okay, so she'd heard of brewer's droop, and had what could well be described as first-hand experience from a couple of old boyfriends - but viticulturist's droop? No, she'd never heard of that, but it was quite clear that in his current condition Brad wasn't going to be of any use to man or beast, but in particular to her.

Despite getting a few hours' sound sleep Brad didn't feel particularly well when he woke up. He initially blamed it on the full-bodied, fifteen per-cent, red wine which Leanne had been plying him with in order to try and get him full-bodied, one hundred per-cent, however in retrospect he realised the manner in which he'd been awoken hadn't been ideal. Just as the last time the phone in the lounge had rung in the middle of the night neither Brad nor Leanne knew exactly what time it was, because just as the last time their bedside clock still wasn't working. And just as Leanne had cursed when she'd previously been awoken by an unwelcome phone call at an unsocial hour, on this occasion she also cursed her husband for not yet having replaced the batteries in that wretched clock.

'Don't worry, I'll get it,' Brad groaned as he pulled back the eiderdown.

'If it's your bloody mother and it's anything less than imminently life-threatening, then you can tell her from me, personally, that she can go and get stuffed.'

Brad sighed. Phone calls in the middle of the night rarely brought good news, but if the caller was Gwen at least it meant that she was still in the land of the living. He lifted the handset but before he had a chance to speak he heard a distinctive greeting which left him in no doubt as to the caller's identity.

'Hello dear. Kissee kissee. I hadn't heard from you for a while so I thought I'd give you a quick call. Now then, before we divulge any personal or sensitive information I need to establish that we are talking on a secure line. Unfortunately I can't see a little padlock on my phone, and the display just says 'Son#1' without the 'https', so I may need to ask you to reset your password.'

Brad sighed again. At least the last time Gwen had called him in the middle of the night she'd waived the security questionnaire.

'You're on the phone Mother, not the Internet, and it's not a good idea to divulge sensitive information over the phone anyway. Now, before we go any further what did you want to talk to me about?'

'Fuck off Gwen,' shouted Leanne from the comfort of the bedroom. 'Don't you know what bloody time it is?'

Gwen clearly heard something of Leanne's demand although evidently not the detail.

'Have you got a woman in there with you Bradley?' she asked. 'Really darling, I'm surprised at you. I wouldn't be surprised at your father of course, but you - well honestly.'

'It's just Leanne. That's my wife Leanne. You know the one?' Brad replied, unable to avoid a touch of sarcasm.

'Oh I see. Her is it? I'd rather hoped she'd left you.'

'I'm sure you do Mother, but I'm very happy to say she's still here. Now then, let's put aside our differences about that particular subject shall we, and you can tell me why you are calling at this unholy hour. Right, here goes -Why have you called me in the middle of the night Mother?'

'Is it really the middle of the night? I lose track of time these days dear. We'd gone to bed and I'd sorted your father out a couple of times – I'm having to deal with him 'manually' shall we say on account of my condition, but he puts on a brave face nevertheless – but then I realised I'd meant to give you a call.'

'So here we are.'

'Exactly.'

Brad couldn't help but feel a combination of regret, sorrow, anger and envy. Regret that he'd failed to ask after his mother's health, sorrow that she was clearly not yet recovered, anger that despite Gwen's illness George still expected his urges to be attended to, and envy that the randy old bastard had still got those urges when he hadn't.'

'So how are you feeling now Mother, and what's been wrong with you anyway?'

'I'd rather not talk about that over the phone Bradley, because it's all rather personal. So what I called to say was why don't you come over to tea tomorrow and I'll let you know the situation. I'd prefer to tell you in person anyway, and I would like my dear George to be there too.'

'So what the fuck does she want at this time of night?' shouted Leanne.

'I'll tell you later Leanne,' Brad called back. 'She's calling about her illness and about, well – going over for tea tomorrow.'

'Shit, I was hoping she was going to tell you she wouldn't make it until tomorrow.'

With that Leanne buried her head underneath her pillow and decided to try and get back to sleep, and let Brad continue the conversation with Gwen until his balls froze off. Oblivious to Leanne's decision to let him continue his conversation unmonitored, and ignoring her comments, Brad wanted to make sure that Gwen was going to be fit to handle the occasion.

'Are you sure you're well enough to do tea tomorrow?'

'Oh, yes dear. I've got some painkillers and some other medicine so I can do a few bits and pieces now. It'll be nice to see you again. Unfortunately your sister may not be able to make it because she's had to go down to Wales or somewhere to collect Frank from a police station. So it may just be the four of us - You, me, George and that girlfriend of yours -whatever her name is - plus Tanya and Gregory.

'Tina and Jeffrey.'

'Yes, them as well dear. We're looking after them for a day or two while Zara is in Wales.'

'No Mother, their names are Tina and Jeffrey, not Tanya and Gregory.'

'I *don't* want to get into an argument at this time of night dear so I'll take your word for it. But I'll have a word with Tanya and Gregory as well.'

\*\*\*

The following day Brad and Leanne drove the few miles over to George and Gwen's bungalow and parked their car on the road outside. Brad had deliberately omitted to mention that Zara might not yet have returned from Wales, knowing that the reason Leanne had consented to tea with his parents in the first place was to pry into his sister's relationship with her wayward partner. Perhaps misguidedly, he chose to reveal the possibility just as Leanne was undoing her seat belt ready to get out of the car.

'Frank appears to have had a bit of a contretemps with a Mr Myfanwy,' Brad explained when Leanne demanded to know why Zara might still be stuck at the western end of the M4. 'And they're probably having to sort the paperwork out in Welsh and, well, you know how long some of those Welsh words are so it'd not be too surprising if she isn't back yet.'

'Who's Mr Myfanwy when he's at home?' replied Leanne, who was pondering whether to throw a hissy-fit and refuse to get out of the car now that her afternoon's entertainment baiting her sister-in-law appeared to have been scuppered.

'You remember that Myfanwy woman Frank had a fling with when he was last down that way? She turns out to have had a husband and he wasn't too chuffed when he discovered that half the Welsh Light Dragoons had been carrying out night manoeuvres around his wife's hidden valleys.'

'But Frank's not in the Light Dragoons,' retorted Leanne, who was beginning to smell a rat. 'He's in the East Anglian.'

'I know, but it appears that Mr Myfanwy had become aware of his wife's penchant for men in uniform after the Welsh Dragoons had been attending to her needs, and had been keeping an eye on her ever since. So when Frank 's indiscretion came to his attention he decided to do something about it. And that's when he and Frank got into a bit of a scrap. Anyway the long and short of it is that Tina and Jeffrey have been staying with Mother and Father while..'

Unfortunately Brad didn't get to finish his sentence because he was interrupted by a loud tapping noise on the car's front driver's side window. Alarmed by the tapping sound and the thought of a revenge-hungry Welshman on the loose, Brad turned his head only to see his mother's face pressed up close to the glass.

'Kissee kissee Bradley dear,' said Gwen, and she moved slightly away from the window and started beckoning her son to leave his car. 'Don't hang about out here getting cold. Come in, come in. I've got something ever so exciting to show you. You can leave that woman in the car or bring her in if you must, it's up to you.'

Brad opened the car door and in next to no time found Gwen virtually dragging him up the garden path and into her bungalow.

'Jeffrey's been showing Granddad how to use a computer, haven't you dear?' Gwen said as she dragged Brad past his nephew and into her dining room. 'In fact he's even given us his old one.'

Leanne looked around the room and quickly spotted an ancient personal computer on a table in the corner. It appeared to be attached to an equally ancient printer.

'So how are you getting on with it then George?' she asked as her father-in-law walked into the room.

'Fucking awful if you really want to know,' replied George. He made the sign of a cross with his two index fingers and pointed his crossed fingers at the computer as if in an attempt to ward off evil spirits.

'He's been doing ever so well, but he hasn't quite got the hang of it all yet, have you George?' said Gwen as she re-emerged from the lounge, unsuccessfully attempting to shepherd her two grand-children into the dining room to say 'Hello' to their Uncle Bradley. George said nothing but blew his nose, and in doing so made a noise that Leanne thought sounded rather like a pig being castrated.

'It wasn't all my fault, was it?'

'What wasn't your fault?' asked Brad.

'Your mother decided to use that new-fangled e-appointment system at the surgery. Have either of you tried to use the damn thing yet?'

Brad shook his head to indicate that neither he nor Leanne had attempted to use Dr Raja's online appointment system.

'Bloody useless load of old crap,' complained George. 'No need to see a real doctor in person, just send them a description or photograph of your ailment and they'll decide if they need to see you. Medicine on the bloody cheap if you ask me, that's what it is.'

'So?'

'So what?'

'So what happened?'

'Well I'd got a bit of a sore spot on my most delicate extremity so I thought I'd better get it checked out, just in case.'

'We thought it best,' added Gwen, superfluously. 'Bearing in mind where he'd been during his wilder days, although he's probably never told me the half of it.'

'I shouldn't think it was anything to worry about,' replied Brad. 'Not unless the incubation period of those particular tropical diseases is over forty years.'

'Exactly son,' replied George, taking hold of Brad's elbow. 'Exactly. But let's not go there, shall we?' he whispered, with a sly wink of his right eye.

'Anyway,' said Gwen. 'Your father took a photo with that new mobile phone of his, and I tried to send it to Dr Raja's e-appointment system for him.'

'What your mother didn't know was that clever young Jeffrey had set up a Twitter account for me - although I'll be buggered if I know what he thought I'd want with one. What's done is done, but somehow I managed to tweet that picture of my meat and two veg to all my followers, complete with my name and address.'

'So how many followers have you got George?' Leanne asked while attempting to suppress her laughter.

'Six at the moment,' George replied with an air of pride in his voice. 'There's that Mrs Ramsbottom woman from number

96 - the one with a face like a battleship – you'd know her if you saw her, believe me. Then there's Alf from the British Legion, Mr and Mrs Hamid from the chip shop - although I think that may be a joint account so perhaps they only count as one – a woman called Svetlana from somewhere in southern Ukraine who says she wants to meet me..'

'And I'm not going to let him,' interrupted Gwen. 'For obvious reasons.'

'And finally Ron from the Off Licence. Not bad for a beginner, eh?'

'Don't forget Jeffrey and Tina dear,' said Gwen, nudging her husband in the side. 'After all, they set up the account for you.'

Although Leanne had just about managed to conceal her amusement at the situation George now found himself in, she'd also spotted the potential for George to find himself in a far more serious predicament.

'So what you're telling us is that you've tweeted a photograph of your cock and balls to your grandson and granddaughter, is that it? Because if it is I think the Social Services might just want to have a few words with you, and sooner rather than later.'

'It's nothing they haven't seen before,' replied Gwen, before George had time to speak. 'I was more worried about the effect it had on Mrs Ramsbottom. Apparently she re-Tweeted it to all her own followers, and then went and printed the photograph out in full colour. And then, if you can believe it, she turned up here the other evening wanting the wretched thing autographed. I mean, the cheek of the woman.'

'Very impressive it was though,' said George with a wide grin on his face. 'Very impressive indeed. Full page, A4 sized portrait. Mind you, it would have looked a damn site better if her printer hadn't been running out of blue ink. Made me look like I'd got a nasty case of jaundice, that it did. If we'd sent that to Dr Raja's bloody e-appointment surgery they'd have me down for a liver transplant by now.'

'And how many followers has Mrs Ramsbottom got?' Brad asked, curious to determine the potential number of copies of his father's apparently jaundiced genitalia there might be floating around the ether.

'Seventeen thousand, nine hundred and eight five,' replied George. 'So I hate to think what she gets up to as a side line.'

'Well, all's well that ends well,' said Brad, now keen to finish this particular conversation, however Gwen wasn't so sure.

'Not really dear. You see some of Mrs Ramsbottom's followers also decided they wanted souvenir copies and followed her example. Queued up to the end of Throgmorton Street they were on Thursday afternoon.'

George grinned again.

'I thought about charging a quid a time. I reckon I'd have made us at least a monkey by the weekend. In fact I felt a bit of a celebrity for a while.'

'Felt a bit of a prick more like,' replied Leanne.

Brad shook his head in disbelief at his father's proposal.

'There are occasions I actually find it hard to believe we're related, let alone that you're my father.' He sighed. 'But putting that aside, what did Doctor Raja say when he saw your little problem?'

'He didn't say anything,' replied George. 'Because it turned out we hadn't sent the photograph to him. I seemed to remember catching the old fella in my zip a couple of days earlier, and the sore spot disappeared anyway. So under the circumstances we decided not to try again in case we ended up putting it on Facebook or something.'

'So all in all not really a great combination, is it? You and technology.'

Brad may have had significant doubts about his father's competence with a computer, but Gwen didn't agree.

'Not at all dear, not at all. Your clever father's been using the computer to write some letters, haven't you dear?'

'What, these?' asked Leanne, as she thumbed through a pile of papers on the table next to George and Gwen's computer, every one of which was addressed to the Chief Executive of a major retailer.

'*Dear Sir or Madam DELETE AS APPROPRIATE*' read Leanne from the top-most letter in the pile.

'*It has come to my attention that your organisation NAME HERE has, over the past few years, been offering incentives to customers on the basis of 'Buy One, Get One Free' or BOGOF.*

'*I write to advise you that I, George Archibald Dixon, first used that acronym to describe an agreement I negotiated with Mr Rajiv Patel of Patel's Gentlemen's Emporium, Kalang Umpor 12, Penang in 1960. I am however minded to allow your organisation NAME HERE to use the aforesaid acronym on payment of a modest fee of £ MONEY HERE.*'

keen on lending it to me either, because they all wanted a go themselves. So by now I'm starting to think that this isn't really going all that well, but just as I'd begun to wonder if the evening was going to have a happy ending for anyone other than the ship's cat, these two women walk in. One's about fifty-five if she's a day, short, with thighs like tree trunks, varicose veins, and a face like a dog's arse with a hat on.'

'What about the other one?' Leanne asked before George had a chance to opine further on the beauties of Chinese womanhood.

'I didn't fancy her half as much actually, but Mr Patel had a proposition for me. *'Forty Ringgit Fucking Tight English with her'* – he points to the dog's arse *'and you get her'* – he points to the other one *'for free'*. You're on, I tell him. That's buy one, get one free – BOGOF. You see?'

His explanation of how he had arrived at the concept of BOGOF decades before the supermarkets completed, George smiled and picked up the pile of letters by which he intended to extract a modest licence fee from some of the world's largest retailers. Brad, however, was not impressed by his father's revelations.

'These are *people* you're talking about Father,' he complained. 'They're not commodities to be traded like they're bags of salt or sugar, or, or anything. They're people with husbands, children and families. They're people who deserve to be treated with respect, with compassion, and with dignity. They're *people* Father, people with human rights.'

George listened to part of Brad's tirade against his father's past indulgences, but interrupted his son before the sermon reached hellfire and damnation.

'Listen, have you ever trekked half way across the Kalahari with just a packet of chocolate digestive and a bottle of your own pee for sustenance? Have you ever spent a month in the deepest jungle, surviving off the land and eating just nuts, twigs and berries?'

'No,' replied Brad. 'I haven't. And neither have you.'

'That's not the point. The point is that if you *had* you'd realise that everything needs to be considered in perspective. Mr Patel was only offering a service for which there was a ready and willing market. And before you get all 'Holier than Thou' with me don't forget it's the world's oldest profession after Tax Inspectors, Estate Agents, Traffic Wardens, and Payment Protection Insurance Claims Handlers. That's just the way it was out there in those days, okay?'

'You're forgetting the arseholes who phone you up every other day preventing to be from your Internet Service Provider,' suggested Leanne. 'You know, the ones who tell you they've detected a problem with your computer and that you need to download some software – Software which would give them access to your bank account. Don't forget those scumbags.'

George looked at Leanne in a manner which suggested he'd not yet encountered the scammers to which Leanne was referring, and for her part Leanne briefly wondered exactly what the scammers might find on George's computer if they ever did infiltrate it.

'So you're expecting these companies to pay you for the use of the BOGOF concept then?' Brad asked once George had finished justifying the most memorable part of his maritime career.

'Some of them at least,' replied George. 'If only ten per cent cough up it'll be worth the effort. All I've got to do now is write in the names of the companies and how much I reckon they ought to be good for, sign them, and pop them in the post. Second Class obviously.'

'You mean these are the final copies?' Leanne asked as she thumbed through the pile of letters.

'Exactly, all I've got to do in fill in those few bits in biro.'

'Why didn't you do a mail merge?'

'A what?'

'A mail merge George. You write one letter leaving out just the bits you need to change on each copy – such as the name and address of the company and its chief executive, and the amount you want to extort, sorry claim – and merge it with a database of the information you need to be inserted in each letter. That way you simply write one letter and merge it with the unique information, and each letter is automatically personalised for you.'

'You mean I didn't need to write each letter individually?'

'No, you could have done them all in one go. You didn't write each one separately, did you George? Tell me you didn't.'

George had fallen silent, and uttered not a single word other than one beginning with 'F'.

'Jeffrey can do it for you dear,' said Gwen, resting her hand gently on her husband's shoulder. 'Can't you Jeffrey?'

Jeffrey nodded. 'Easy-peasy Gran.'

'Fucking technology,' muttered George. 'Just think of all the time I could have saved if only I'd known.'

'I wouldn't worry too much about it,' said Leanne, as she noticed a number of spelling mistakes in the letters. 'You're retired so all you're doing is hanging around in heaven's waiting room anyway.'

'Bloody cheek,' grumbled George. Leanne turned to look at Gwen and delivered what she might have expected to be her *coup de grace*. 'Or Hell's in your case.'

Much to Leanne's surprise, Gwen failed to respond to Leanne's poisoned bait in much the same way that Zoe had failed to react to the gibe about her red shoes equating to a lack of underwear. In fact Gwen simply nodded and muttered 'Only time will tell' making Leanne wonder if she was losing the knack of winding up her mother-in-law, or for that matter women in general.

'Only time will tell,' repeated Gwen, louder this time. 'I've not led a blameless life perhaps, but I've tried to be a good wife and mother, and grandmother. I've got two wonderful children, and they're all grown up and married..'

'Mummy's not married,' interrupted Tina. 'She was married once but she's not anymore.'

'Well she's got Frank, and Bradley's got, well..' Gwen looked back at Leanne.

'I should think he'd be delighted,' Derek replied, although he failed to mention the recent minor confrontation between the two men. 'After all, he can't technically act on our behalf due to him being employed by the local Council, and the last time I mentioned it to him I got the distinct impression he regarded the whole thing as a pain in the bum.'

'So she's fully qualified, is she? This new planning consultant you're proposing?'

'From what I understand she's every bit as well qualified as Brad is.'

'That's a fat lot of comfort,' said Alison. 'Bearing in mind all the hassle he's caused us with these damn log cabins. What with log cabins *technically* being caravans, and caravans not being caravans unless they can be moved from place to place in not more than two pieces, and all the rest of that legal stuff he tried to explain to us one day. I still can't make head or tail of it.'

Despite Alison's concerns Derek was keen to move onto the next item on the agenda, namely that of the Club's appointed planning consultant also being authorised to act on the Club's behalf.

'Notwithstanding Anna and Alison's representations I'm assuming we're otherwise content that Zoe be appointed as our planning consultant and also that she be authorised to deal with the local Council on planning matters?'

There was a show of hands as a result of which Zoe was elevated from humble applicant to 'Bronze' club member and Planning Consultant-in-Chief in one fell swoop. Geoffrey was just about to move onto the next item on the agenda when Louise decided that Anna's efforts to increase membership were worthy of note, particularly bearing in mind her near tantrum at the previous meeting.

'So Anna's initiative gained us at least one new member, and I think we should recognise that, don't you?'

There were general mutterings of approval of Anna's initiative, and her efforts were duly recorded in the Minutes along with the fact that another member had recently resigned, resulting in a net gain of zero in membership numbers, and a net loss in terms of membership fees as the resigning member had been due a refund.

'So precisely what is the financial situation Derek?' Anna asked, fully expecting the club's Treasurer to be hopelessly ill-equipped to provide an answer.

'That's later on the agenda if you don't mind,' replied Geoffrey, which at least gave Derek pre-warning that he might be expected to have that kind of information to hand.

'In general terms then?'

'About the same as it was, plus or minus,' said Derek.

'So on that basis the club is no better placed to obtain any further log cabins anyway.'

'Well actually that's where you're wrong Anna.'

Having managed to deflect Anna's criticism for once in his life, Derek went on to explain what Zoe had told him about the club's Planning Permission being for the benefit of the land, rather than the club itself. More impressively perhaps he managed to convey the information correctly.

'So you mean any of the club's members could put a log cabin on the land?' asked Alison.

'Exactly, with the club's permission of course.'

'So Steve and I could have one?'

'Yes, if you can afford it, and the club's site rental fee of course.'

Each of the Committee members could see where this discussion was heading, and it was heading in the direction of those present working out if they and their husbands, wives or partners could afford a log cabin of their own - together with the club's site rental fee - whatever that might turn out to be. One of the Committee members was also wondering if they and somebody else's wife, husband or partner might rather like their own private love nest in the club's grounds but didn't say as much.

'The point is,' said Derek once his mind had returned to the committee meeting and away from the rather enticing fantasy of a few nights in a log cabin with Zoe and her oscillating arse. 'The point is that the club could get a decent income from renting out sites for those log cabins, the same way we get income from 'Gold' members for their camping rights. We'd have to charge them more, obviously, but you can see the potential for an increase in capital at no cost to the club.'

'Revenue,' said Anna. 'Money coming in like that is called 'Revenue', not 'Capital'.'

'Alright then, an increase in revenue at no cost to the club.'

'I'd really prefer '*An increase in revenue without any capital expenditure*' if this is going in the Minutes,' said Geoffrey. 'But you were the banker Derek, not me.'

With the club's finances in a particularly precarious situation there was little doubt that the Committee would resolve to allow its members to put log cabins in the club's grounds, thus getting them ever closer to the massive bun fight Brad had predicted.

'Well I think we should propose a vote of thanks to Brad,' said Anna. 'After all, he got us permission for the log cabins in the first place whether we wanted them or not, and now we've gone and sacked the poor bugger for his trouble.'

The Committee members all raised their hands and Brad was duly thanked, *in absentia*, for his previous efforts.

'Talking of the Dixons,' said Anna. 'Isn't it sad news about Gwen?'

'It is indeed,' replied Geoffrey. 'Brad told me about her the other day. No wonder she hasn't been about recently. I didn't like to pry. You don't, do you?'

The Committee agreed that they didn't like to pry, about some things at least, although the fact was not recorded in the Minutes.

'I wonder how George will cope,' said Anna.

The Committee members all paused for a moment to wonder how George would cope, and indeed how they, too, might cope were they to find themselves in a similar situation.

'Do we know how long?' asked Derek.

'To be honest I didn't like to ask,' replied Geoffrey. 'You don't, do you?'

The Committee agreed that they didn't like to ask, in much the same way they'd agreed they didn't like to pry, although again the matter was not recorded in the Minutes.

'Shall we turn to lighter matters?' asked Geoffrey.

'I wonder if poor old Brad will ever be able to get wood again?' said Derek with a grin, much to Geoffrey's annoyance.

'Perhaps I'll have a quiet word with Leanne the next time I see her,' replied Anna. 'After all, we need to know these things, don't we girls?'

# Chapter 13

Brad realised he hadn't been paying attention to what Leanne had been saying when they'd been driving home from George and Gwen's place. He'd been paying so little attention in fact that he hadn't realised they'd taken a wrong turning, and had ended up going around the one-way system in the town centre. In hindsight Brad's lack of attention on that occasion wasn't really surprising, and also in hindsight Brad had realised that it might have been wiser to have let Leanne drive that evening, even though her driving did scare the crap out of him. Indicators were invented for a purpose, after all, as was the clutch. Perhaps if Gwen had been more direct it wouldn't have affected him the same way. If she'd simply said 'I'm sorry to have to tell you all that I've got cancer' Brad might have dealt with that news – terrible though it was – later in private contemplation. But Gwen hadn't done that. Instead she'd dropped her bombshell as a casual aside while Tina was reciting a list of new words she could now spell thanks to her school and its wretched spelling exercise.

'We've been doing signs of the Zodiac this week Granddad,' Tina proudly announced, to which George replied that it'd be a bloody sight more use the school teaching her to spell 'arse' than 'Aries', let alone 'Sagittarius'.

'A-R-I-E-S spells Aries Grandma.'

'Yes dear,' Gwen replied. 'Very good dear.'

'So what did Doctor Raja say is wrong with you Mother?' Brad asked in-between Gwen acknowledging Tina's ability to correctly spell both 'Pisces' and 'Leo'.

'Well Bradley, I've got..' Gwen paused for a moment and looked pensive. 'Do you know I've gone and forgotten what it's called? What was it now? It begins with a C.'

'C-A-N-C-E-R spells Cancer,' said Tina.

'Yes dear, that's it.'

Tina had managed to work her way through Aquarius, Virgo and Gemini by the time Brad managed to mumble the question 'Can they operate?'

'No dear. I'm afraid nature's got to take its course. I've got some painkillers but otherwise it's just a matter of time.'

'How long?'

'A few weeks dear, maybe a couple of months. Doctor Raja said they can never be sure, especially in someone of my age.'

Brad said nothing more than 'I'm so sorry,' but he hadn't been sure whether or not Gwen had heard him, because Tina had misspelt 'Capricorn' by using a 'K' and Gwen had been busy correcting her. Leanne certainly noticed Brad's reaction to his mother's news, because she took both Brad's hands in her own and squeezed them tightly, which was a distinct change from the parts Leanne had most recently been used to squeezing in an attempt to find out if there was any sign of life within.

'It's a bit of a bugger all this,' George said, in what Brad had regarded as a massive understatement, but one he chose not to challenge.

'We'll be down at the Hidden Lake from time to time,' George had told Brad as he and Leanne prepared to leave for home. 'When the weather's a bit warmer and your mother feels like it, that is.'

'Just let us know if you'd like a lift, to save you having to go all the way there on those shopping scooters of yours, won't you? Or if there's anything else the pair of you need. Anything at all, just say. Okay? Just let us know. We'll be there to do whatever you need from us. You only have to ask.'

George graciously accepted the offer of help on Gwen's behalf. It was a kind offer and one he'd felt sure his son would make. What he hadn't expected was that it would come from his daughter in law, and neither for that matter had Brad, particularly bearing in mind just how acrimonious the relationship between his wife and mother had been recently.

\*\*\*

It may have been that Brad's mind had been so preoccupied with both Gwen's news and Leanne's reaction to it that he'd taken that wrong turn in a route he'd driven countless times before. It may also have been so preoccupied that he hadn't even heard Leanne issue a warning about his imminent blunder, let alone do anything to prevent it. Whatever the reason it wasn't until Brad and Leanne were safely out of the one-way system and set on a course for home that Brad eventually spoke, although when the silence was broken it wasn't only Gwen's news that he wanted to talk about.

'Thank you for offering to help Mother and Father out. I was going to but I.., well, I didn't really know what to say. I, er, I hadn't really taken it all in to be honest. It all came as such a shock.'

'Don't worry about that right now sweetheart. Just let's get home safe and sound shall we? And then we can talk about it if you want.'

Brad nodded his head and began to ask a question, but before he got more than half way through Leanne answered it for him.

'Okay, but tell me one thing..'

'Why did I offer to help?'

'Well, yes. The pair of you have never exactly seen eye to eye, have you? And ever since that time Mother laced your tea with laxatives and got you subjected to an intimate body search at Heathrow you've really had it in for each other.'

Leanne turned her head away from her husband to look out of the car's side window, which would have made it difficult for him to hear what she was about to say, but she turned back to face him before she eventually began to speak.

'I saw a look on your face if you want to know. A look that said you're afraid of losing something really precious. After all, she bore you for nine months – ten and a half months if you believe her, which to be honest I never have – and all that time, and ever since, she's been there for you. And then I arrive on the scene and she realises that her little boy has all grown up, and suddenly she's afraid of losing you to another woman.'

'So who'd that be then?' Brad asked, trying to suppress a grin.

'Very funny. You told me before she didn't like your other girlfriends, not that there were many - or so I gather – so I don't suppose she's treated me any differently to the rest of them. It's just that unlike the others I didn't dump you, and then we got married and you moved away from home, and I think she probably blames me for that. Anyway, what's done is done, and it's all in the past. We don't know how long she's got left, so I'm going to do everything I can to make her final months or weeks as enjoyable as possible, even if I do have to grit my teeth on occasions.'

Brad would probably have tried to lean across the car and kiss Leanne on the cheek if he hadn't been attempting to negotiate a roundabout at the time. Instead he just thanked her and told her how much it meant to him that she'd finally decided not only to signal an end to hostilities and call a truce with Gwen, but that she'd decided to make unilateral amends for all their previous unpleasantness towards each other. With a maelstrom of thoughts, fears and questions whirling around in his brain, Brad took some comfort from what Leanne had just told him. He fully believed that Leanne's decision had come from the heart, although any thoughts she might have been harbouring about her husband's relationship with another woman with long blonde hair, red shoes and no knickers never even crossed his mind.

DJ Vic handed the microphone over to Derek who had been standing behind him on the stage.

'Thank you Vic. Before we start I'd just like to stress that that the winners of the draw are only being offered to *right* to buy a log cabin and to site it within the club's grounds. They're not getting the cabin themselves, not for a tenner. Now, the way the draw will work is as follows: The first six names drawn will automatically get the option to buy one of the log cabins, which is to be occupied by the winners themselves. Occupation of the said cabin by any other person or persons will incur a camping fee at the club's normal daily rate. Is that clear? Good. We will also be drawing a further three names, who will get the option to buy a cabin in the event that any of the first six winners decline their option, or fail to pay in full, or otherwise fail to meet their obligations in respect of said offer. If the offer to that further group fails to result in the sale of all the cabins then a further draw will be held at our next social event or such date in the future as the Committee in its sole discretion shall decide. Is that all clear too?'

'Just get on with it,' shouted a voice from the back of the clubhouse.

'Right then,' said Derek. 'I'll now hand you over to Louise to make the grand draw.'

'Why doesn't he just do the sodding draw and be done with it?' said the voice from the back of the clubhouse who had previously demanded that Derek get on with it.

'Thank you Derek,' said Louise as she took the microphone from her Committee colleague's hand. 'In this biscuit tin there's an envelope containing a slip of paper for each family who are

'Gold' club members and who have paid £10 to be included in the draw. The first six envelopes to be drawn will contain the names of the winning families who will automatically be offered the right to buy a log cabin.'

'Have I got time to go and have a pee, or are you going to be making the draw anytime soon?' came the now familiar voice from the back of the clubhouse.

'You didn't buy a ticket Ralph so you can go and have a shit for all I care,' replied Louise. 'Right, it's time to draw the first lucky winner. I'm going to ask one of our oldest and dearest members to draw the first envelope. As we all know, Gwen has been very poorly lately, but I'm delighted to say she's well enough to join us this evening. So on behalf of all of us I'd like to say how nice it is to see you again Gwen, and wish you well for a speedy recovery.'

Gwen didn't know what to say. She hadn't been expecting to be asked to make the draw, and she certainly hadn't expected Derek to hand her a bunch of carnations and kiss her on the cheek. That was a lovely thing to do, she thought, even if the carnations did still have the price label on, and that it had been over-stamped with a label saying 'Oops. Now £1.40.'

Louise held out the biscuit tin containing the envelopes so that Gwen could pick the first winner. Gwen shut her eyes, put her hand into the biscuit tin, stirred the envelopes around a little and then pulled one out.

'And the winner is..' said Louise as she took the envelope from Gwen's hand. 'Alison and Steve.'

There was a brief round of applause which drowned a cry of 'Oh yes!' from Steve when he realised he and his partner had won the right to buy the first of the six piles of wood standing just to one side of the club's car park. One or two of those present also realised that the first names to be drawn were those of a Committee member and her partner, but none chose to say it out loud.

'Would you draw the next envelope please Alison,' said Louise as she held out the biscuit tin in front of another Committee member.

Alison shut her eyes and drew out the second envelope and passed it to Louise.

'And the second winner is.. Geoffrey.'

There was another brief round of applause, less prolonged or generous than the first, and it didn't quite mask the murmurings of 'Bloody fixed' from the rear of the room.

'And if you would do the honours please Geoffrey.'

Geoffrey stretched his arm out, drew the third winning envelope out of the biscuit tin, and passed it to Louise.

'And the winner is.. Well I never! That *is* a surprise.'

There was even less applause than when Geoffrey's name had been pulled out of the biscuit tin, together with distinct rumblings of 'Fixed.'

'I can assure you the fact that the last three envelopes drawn all contained the names of Committee members is a complete co-incidence. But as I don't feel it would be fair to draw the next envelope myself I'm going to ask Gwen to take another envelope on my behalf.'

Gwen stuck her hand into the biscuit tin, shut her eyes for a second time, and pulled out another envelope.

'Brad and Leanne,' announced Louise, to which there was loud applause and a shriek of delight from Leanne who flung her arms around her mother-in-law and kissed her on both cheeks.

'I wonder how many of the Committee she had to sleep with for *that* to happen,' shouted Ralph, a remark which - if anybody had heard him - would have landed Ralph an appointment with the Committee to explain himself.

With the excitement of winning Leanne found herself struggling to regain her composure, but even with her hand trembling she managed to pull an envelope containing the names 'Alice and Paul' out of the biscuit tin. Alice and Paul were also popular winners, if only because neither were Committee members. Unfortunately Alice didn't do quite such a popular job when she drew Derek as the last of the six winning names, but as two of the winners had turned out *not* to be Committee members those crying foul should have wondered if their allegations would stand scrutiny. The fact that none of the remaining Committee members had actually bought tickets was, of course, irrelevant.

'I think we should have independent verification of the winners,' shouted Ralph. 'Because I'm not satisfied with the way that draw was handled.'

'Are you suggesting that the draw was fixed Ralph?' asked Louise. 'Because if you are that's a very serious allegation.'

'I'm just saying, that's all.'

Louise walked to the centre of the dance floor brandishing the six slips of paper on which were written the names of the lucky winners.

'Alison and Steve,' she said, reading the names on the uppermost slip of paper, before letting the paper fall to the floor. 'Alison and Steve, Geoffrey, Louise, Brad and Leanne, Alice and Paul, and Derek. There you are Ralph. Now, how about you come here and pick up those pieces of paper and read them out for yourself, and then tell me if you're not satisfied.'

Ralph made his way from the far side of the clubhouse until he reached the spot where Louise was standing. Then he bent over and picked up the slips of paper.

'Read them.'

'Brad and Leanne, Alison and Steve, Derek, Geoffrey, Louise, Alice and Paul.'

'Thank you Ralph. So now are you satisfied?'

Ralph said that he was satisfied, and that there had never been any suggestion of impropriety. The draw just needed to be verified, that was all.

'Good,' replied Louise. 'Because despite the fact that the winning slips need to be retained for the club's records, if there had been any suggestion of wrong-doing I'd have happily rolled them up very tight, and the next time I caught you face down on a sun lounger I'd have shoved them quite vigorously where the sun don't shine.'

His tail well and truly between his legs Ralph made his way back to his table.

'That was bloody close,' Louise thought to herself as she made her way to the ladies' lavatory. 'Bloody close, but better safe than sorry.'

It had been bloody close, but Louise allowed herself the briefest of smiles before stuffing the six winning slips into her handbag, along with the six unopened envelopes that had been drawn out of a biscuit tin just a few minutes earlier. There would be no need to draw a further three names as had been originally proposed, because none of the winners would want to miss out on the chance to secure themselves a log cabin. In hindsight that was probably just as well, because if any of the winners were to be drawn a second time there would be some serious explaining to do. Louise had taken care of most eventualities, but that was one she'd missed.

***

The rest of the evening went with a swing and was enjoyed by all, apart possibly by those 'Gold' members whose names had not been pulled out of Louise's biscuit tin. DJ Vic was in fine form, and played hits past and present to which many of the club's members were eager to dance. Gwen had particularly enjoyed her gin and tonic, so when Brad and Leanne returned to their table from the dance floor she asked Brad if he would go and mix her another. It had been thoughtful, too, of Leanne to bring along a selection of canapés to share, especially as she'd insisted that Gwen take the breaded prawns of which she knew Gwen was particularly fond.

The music may not have been to George's taste, but with Gwen firmly seated for the evening he happily made his way around the room, flirting outrageously with as many women as he could, and grabbing a dance with the younger ones every time DJ Vic put on a record he could smooch to. And if Gwen and George were enjoying themselves, Brad and Leanne were all the more so. With the right to buy a log cabin secured Brad no longer had any need to put up a tent for the remainder of the summer season. Moreover – and this was something that had occurred to both Brad and Leanne – with peace, tranquillity and some quality time spent together in a log cabin, it might just get Brad's errant member moving in a northerly direction, and possibly even keep it there for more than fifteen seconds at a time. Finally for Leanne it was a dream come true. The thrill she'd experienced the moment she realised she'd got a winning ticket was the closest she'd come to a multiple orgasm since Brad lost his ability to even start to meet her needs. In hindsight - and the more Leanne thought about it - it was probably as close as she'd come to a multiple orgasm since before she'd even met Brad. In fact probably since a particularly eventful Christmas office party when she'd drunk far too much, had met a charming young Frenchman, and had woken up the next morning locked in the broom cupboard. Still, the less said about that the better. Some things should remain on a strictly 'need to know' basis, and Brad certainly didn't. All things considered it could have been the perfect evening, and it might well have been had one particularly bad penny not turned up to spoil the fun.

# Chapter 18

Zoe never liked driving to London, and almost half an hour stuck on the A12 near Chelmsford hadn't made the journey to the Hidden Lake Club any more pleasant. By the time she arrived Zoe had already missed the grand draw for the log cabins, although she had no particular interest in it as she wasn't eligible to take part anyway. She parked her car, turned off the headlights and the ignition, swore to herself about the traffic hold-ups and the appalling state of the A12 near Ingatestone, and then put on a happy face and some lipstick ready to go and join the party. Zoe had just got out of her car and was about to walk the short distance to the clubhouse when a thought crossed her mind. In view of the club's 'Naked after Nine' policy should she leave her underwear on or take it off? Zoe decided on the latter, so she walked back to her car, took off her blouse and skirt, and then put her bra and knickers over the steering wheel as an *aide-memoire* for when she left. A couple of the club's members saw her standing next to her car stripping off but just waved to her and called out 'Hi Zoe'. There was nothing remotely unusual about wandering around a naturist club's car park naked, and on more than one occasion club members had driven as far as the club's entrance gates before realising they weren't dressed for the occasion, although it had prompted a number of questions including where they'd the hell they'd kept the car keys.

The clubhouse was crowded that evening, and as she looked around the darkened room the only spare seat Zoe could see was one next to Brad. That suited her just fine, after all Brad was an old friend and she didn't really know that many of the club's other members particularly well yet anyway. Zoe didn't actually need to ask if she could join the Dixon party, because just as soon as George saw her standing by the entrance door he ended his conversation with one of the club's more elderly women and made a beeline for the more up to date model. Despite George's worst intentions Zoe ended up sitting next to Brad which suited the pair of them if not George, and especially not Leanne. Before long Brad and Zoe were engaged in a deep discussion about the legal status of the six piles of timber that were currently sitting next to the club's car park, and how Zoe had come to the conclusion that they could still technically be classed as 'Caravans'.

'Read *The Caravan Sites Act 1968* in detail.' Zoe trilled while Brad shook his head from side to side. 'You know as well as I do that Act amended the 1960 *Caravan Sites and Control of Development Act* to include twin-unit caravans. If you read Section 13(1)(b) you'll see it makes it perfectly clear that they only need to be *capable* of being moved. I can't remember the exact wording, but it's to the effect that a unit 'composed of not more than two sections separately constructed and designed to be assembled on a site by means of bolts, or screws, or nuts', or something or other - and 'is when assembled capable of being moved by road from one place to another shall not be treated as not being - or as not having been - a caravan under the 1960 Act by reason only that it cannot lawfully be moved on a highway when put together'. Oh, how I bloody well hate those double negatives, don't you? Whatever, when those log cabins are assembled they'll be just that, and therefore *legally* they'll be caravans, even if you think they aren't at present - which they are - and which they were before they were dismantled.'

'You seem to be overlooking one minor point,' retorted Brad. 'Namely that under the 1960 Act 'Caravan' refers to means any structure designed or adapted for human habitation which is capable of being moved from one place to another. Those piles of timber, in their current form, do not appear to me to be designed for *human* habitation. By Great Crested Newts, perhaps, but not by humans. See Section 29(1) of the 1960 Act about that. So what we have here is a situation where we don't *know* one way or another if those piles of wood, when assembled, *would* form a unit capable of being moved in not more than two pieces. Similarly, we don't *know* whether the assembled units *were* designed for human habitation in the first place. Even allowing for the fact that you only need to demonstrate your argument on the 'Balance of Probability' rather than 'Beyond Reasonable Doubt' as would be the case in criminal law, I would suggest we are simply not in a position to form an opinion one way or the other. On that basis your argument that they *are* caravans can only fail because the bottom line is that it's not possible to say.'

'Let's call it a draw then, shall we?'

'Sorry Zoe. No. As far as establishing lawfulness is concerned the onus is on *you* to demonstrate your case, *not* on me to disprove it.'

Zoe laughed. 'You always were a bloody pedantic pain in the arse Brad. But whether or not those piles of timber are, or are not, legally caravans didn't stop you wanting one, did it? No, it didn't. Anyway, whether or not the club's bought six caravans in the form of log cabins or not, the simple fact is that they'll be sitting in the club's private grounds, and shielded from prying eyes by acres of woodlands and a damn great fence topped with barbed wire, not to mention a blackthorn hedge behind. So whether they are now - or will legally become - caravans once assembled or not, the bottom line is that nobody apart from you and me is going to know. And we aren't going to say anything, are we?'

Zoe smiled and grabbed Brad's right hand before issuing a demand that would have set alarm bells ringing in Leanne's ears if she'd heard it.

'C'mon Brad, get yourself up and onto that dance floor. Let's get you all hot and sweaty.'

Just as at the Valentine's dance Brad protested that it wasn't really his kind of music, and that he really didn't 'do' dancing, but once again Zoe persisted and a couple of minutes later the pair of them were shaking their hips and their arms and their legs sufficiently in time with the music for their efforts to be classified as 'freestyle' rather than St Vitus. The standard three minutes for a hit 'pop' song was soon over, but DJ Vic skilfully mixed the final few bars of the last up-tempo number with the soothing rhythm of a slow ballad. Brad was ready to go and sit down with the rest of the Dixon family but Zoe had other ideas, and grabbing her former colleague by the hand pulled their bodies tightly together.

'I love this song Brad,' Zoe cooed, squeezing Brad closer still. 'It makes me feel so romantic. I just want make love every time I hear it. Leanne won't mind will she?'

Brad blushed, but he managed to interpret Zoe's question to mean whether or not Leanne would mind the pair of them dancing cheek-to-cheek rather than anything else. In fact Leanne didn't mind because she was looking the other way, and was busy talking to Gwen. Just as she had been the previous day,

Gwen was having a wonderful time. She'd had a lovely chat with some of her best friends, her darling son had mixed her a couple of very nice gin and tonics, she'd been assured by Leanne that her daughter-in-law wouldn't steal Brad from her, and that Brad would always be his mother's son and would always love her. George was also getting well into the swing of things, and was gradually working his way through a long mental list of the women he wanted to try and chat up before the night was over. Brad even seemed to be enjoying himself, having engaged in a pedantic battle of wits regarding the finer points of planning law - a topic which Leanne had told Gwen left her stone cold. And now Brad was – Leanne looked around the room, suddenly aware that her husband wasn't sitting next to her, and had been absent far too long to suggest he'd simply gone off to have a pee. Where the hell was he? Brad was squeezed tightly against that wretched Zoe woman, that's where Brad was. Squeezed tightly against a body whose hips were slowly and sensuously swaying back and forth in time with the music. Leanne suddenly felt a sense of foreboding despite the fact that so far she'd really been enjoying the evening. She'd secured the peace with her mother-in-law, had evaded George's advances, and had enjoyed a couple of nice glasses of wine. In fact she was still tingling from the effects of her earlier close encounter with a multiple orgasm, so all in all it hadn't been a bad evening. Now, however, Leanne found herself keeping a very close eye on her husband – his hands in particular - and those of that bloody tart Zoe. One thing was for sure, if there was the merest hint of distortion in the front of Brad's trousers once the tart released him from her clutches there would be hell to pay.

Oblivious to the fact that Leanne had realised he was dancing with Zoe, and also to her decision to inspect the shape of his trousers upon return from the dance floor, Brad was also enjoying the evening. He felt he'd won the academic battle regarding the provisions of the 1960 Act with Zoe, had secured the right to acquire a pile of logs – even if *technically* they didn't constitute a caravan in their current form - and was in the company of his family, friends and lover. The only problem as far as the latter two were concerned was that Brad wasn't entirely sure which was which.

# Chapter 19

It must have been around four o'clock in the morning when the phone in Brad and Leanne's lounge rang. Brad couldn't be entirely sure what time it was because the bedside clock still didn't have any batteries in it. He hadn't forgotten about them, and to help him Leanne had provided a handy aide-memoire by writing 'Batteries for the bedside clock' on a piece of paper and pinning it to a cork notice board in the kitchen. Unfortunately the batteries Brad bought had turned out to be the wrong size but had not gone to waste because Leanne had commandeered them, having discovered they were the size she required for another important piece of portable electrical apparatus that had been getting far more use than it had been designed for since Brad's organic equivalent had gone tits up. Brad answered the phone, fully expecting it to be one of his parents, but which one and the nature of the call was really not something he could take for granted these days.

'Hello dear, kissee kissee,' said the voice on the other end of the phone. 'Have I reached the household of Mr Bradley Dixon, only son of Mrs Gwen Dixon and Mr George Dixon?'

'Yes Mother, you have. What is it? Are you okay?'

'Yes dear, I'm fine thank you. Now, before we go any further I need to ask you some security questions. This call may also be recorded for quality and training purposes.'

Brad didn't bother to argue, knowing that to do so would prolong the call inexorably.

'Is that Gwen?' called Leanne from the bedroom.

'Yes.'

'Is she okay? What's the problem?'

'She's fine. I'm not sure what she wants yet, but we're back to the old security question routine, so that may or may not be a good sign.'

'Now then dear,' said Gwen. 'Here is the first question – What is your wife's name?'

'Leanne,' replied Brad, surprised that Gwen would involve her in what she clearly regarded as a matter of some importance.

'What?' replied Leanne.

'No, not you.'

'Well which Leanne then? Or did you mean Zoe? Because if you did and I ever hear you mumbling her name when you're asleep I'll cut your dick off. It's no use to me and hasn't been for some time now - as well you know - but believe me I'll make bloody sure it's no use to her either.'

'And here is your second question dear,' said Gwen, oblivious to the nature of the conversation unfolding at the Dixon junior household.

'On what date were you married?'

'I, er,' Brad paused to think. 'I can't quite remember at the moment.'

'What does she want to know?' asked Leanne.

'Oh, er, just a date.'

'Well if the answer is either the May 18th or the October 1st and you've forgotten either of them I'll cut your fucking balls off as well.'

Brad briefly wondered why he and Leanne hadn't married on some date that was easier to remember – for some reason the first of April sprung to mind – but he was reluctant to give Gwen the correct answer lest he should unwittingly then mutter another woman's name when Leanne had a sharp implement to hand.

'October 22nd, 1805,' said Brad, giving the first date that came into his mind, and making sure he spoke loudly enough for Leanne to hear. 'The day after the Battle of Trafalgar.'

'Thank you dear,' replied Gwen. 'That's not quite right, but I think under the circumstances it's probably close enough.'

Brad breathed a sigh of relief in the knowledge that his gonads were once again relatively safe.

'Good, now what are you calling about?'

'It's those numbers Bradley dear. You know, the number of pieces of wood and their sizes. The bits and bobs you need to make those six log cabins.'

'What about them?'

'They don't add up dear, even on Tina and Jeffrey's new computer, and they should. After all, that computer can do millions of sums every second, and that's a lot more than George or I can do even with a calculator.'

Gwen explained how she'd e-mailed her list of numbers and sizes to her grand-children, following the instructions that Leanne had written down for her. Much to Gwen's surprise,

Jeffrey and Tina had received the e-mail, complete with Gwen's detailed list of the various components she and Leanne had measured in the club's car park. But try as they might neither Jeffrey nor Tina could work out which pieces were needed to make a 'Windsor' or a 'Buckingham' log cabin, despite having downloaded further details of the cabins from 'Meritorious Sheds' website themselves.

'That's not fair Grandma,' Tina had complained when Gwen called her to find out how the calculations were progressing. 'You gave us an impossible puzzle. We took it to school and let the teachers look at it, and they couldn't solve it either. It's a complete swizz. And tell Granddad his spelling only scored 3 out of 20. My teacher said she'd never even heard of some of the words he spelt. And some of them "Shouldn't ever be used in polite company," I think she said.'

Gwen briefly waited to see if Brad could offer any suggestions as to why the piles of timber currently residing in the Hidden Lake Club's car park didn't seem to be capable of being re-assembled into either of two types of log cabin. Unsurprisingly he couldn't, and although he thought he understood what Gwen was trying to say, he struggled to understand why she'd chosen to call him at that particular hour about the subject.

'I wanted to let you know before I forgot again dear. I spoke to Tina and Jeffrey when they got home from school this afternoon but it must have slipped my mind until just now. I didn't want to risk forgetting it again, so here we are.'

Brad hadn't been particularly happy to have been woken up at some silly hour, but at least on this occasion Gwen had something important to say, in fact so important it would necessitate a further meeting of the Hidden Lake Club's executive Committee.

'Thank Leanne again for the tea and nibbles the other evening, won't you Bradley? And give her my love. Kissee kissee.'

Brad replied that he would give Leanne Gwen's love, and when he got back to their bedroom he would have done exactly that if she hadn't been fast asleep.

# Chapter 20

It was far too important a subject to wait until the next scheduled meeting of the Hidden Lake Club's executive Committee, but nevertheless Anna, Derek and the others were not best pleased to be summoned to discuss the small matter of the log cabins with their former planning consultant.

'So what *exactly* are you saying Brad?' Anna asked just as soon as Geoffrey had opened the meeting.

'They're not all there,' Brad replied, to which Anna responded that if he was referring to Derek's brain cells then tell her something she didn't already know.

'Those carava - those piles of timber we unloaded the other day. There aren't enough pieces to make six cabins, not three 'Windsors' and three 'Buckinghams' anyway. In fact, from what my niece and nephew worked out there's about forty per cent missing.'

'Can you explain this Derek?' asked Geoffrey. 'Are another three lorries going to turn up with the remainder of the pieces?'

Derek replied that he didn't know, although he had a sneaking suspicion he knew what the problem was.

'I'll have to make a phone call to my business partner,' he said, as several sets of piercing eyes locked their Treasurer firmly in their sights.

Derek took his mobile phone out of his pocket and ran his finger down his list of contacts. He 'tut-tutted' loudly. 'Bloody mobile coverage out here's still crap' he complained once he'd retrieved the number he was looking for. 'One damn bar out of five, can you believe that? I'll have to try and see if it's any better in the car park.'

Derek got up and went out into the car park to make his phone call. He'd got some quick thinking to do, and it would be far easier if he was able to do it without the rest of the Committee breathing down his neck. He'd always known he'd taken a risk with those log cabins, it was just fortunate that none of the Committee had noticed the signal strength reading on his mobile phone had been reading five out of five.

Ten minutes later Derek returned to the meeting, and proudly announced that he'd negotiated a £250 discount on each of the cabins to make up for the fact that there were a few pieces missing. He'd actually done no such thing, but circumstances meant that his own profit margin would have to take a hit.

'So where are the rest of the timbers Derek?' Geoffrey asked just as soon as his Treasurer had explained everything else he said he knew.

'Well, it depends really,' came the reply, as Derek tried his utmost to avoid answering the question.

'On what?'

'Oh, all sorts of stuff.'

'Such as?'

'Well, for a start there's tidal flow, currents, wind speed and direction, and so on. Factors which as I'm sure you will understand are all beyond the control of mere mankind, let alone that of your humble Treasurer.'

'Let me put it another way then Derek,' said Anna who was starting to get suspicious. 'Where do you think they are? The missing timbers, that is.'

'Probably somewhere between Lowestoft and Zeebrugge, although I suppose some bits might be as far south as Margate by now. It's difficult to be more precise.'

'Do you mean to say the rest of our cabins are lost somewhere in the North Sea Derek?' asked Geoffrey.

'Well it's a lot bigger than it looks on a map so it's really quite easy to lose things in it, but in short – Yes.'

Geoffrey wasted no further time and demanded a full explanation. The Hidden Lake Club, as far as he was concerned, had ordered and presumably paid for six log cabins, and had subsequently sold the rights to buy the said log cabins for the benefit of – well, mostly the benefit of the Committee really, but that wasn't the point. Anna, too, wanted a full explanation.

'You told us you'd bought six second-hand log cabins Derek. So now you're telling us you bought six piles of driftwood. Is that it?'

Derek replied that it wasn't. He had ordered six second hand cabins – or 'pre-loved cabins' as he put it – three each of the 'Buckingham' and the 'Windsor'.

'Remember that tidal surge last winter? You can't have forgotten what a stormy night that was. The caravans were right on the cliff edge, and when the cliff finally gave way part of those caravans went over the edge.'

'And you bought all the scrap wood from the bottom of the cliff?'

'No, I bought what was left standing on the top. But before you all attempt to rip me to shreds let me explain. Do you remember what Brad and Zoe were going on about caravans being transportable in not more than two pieces?'

The other members of the Committee could hardly have forgotten. Firstly Brad had confused the hell out of the lot of them with his pseudo-legalese mumbo jumbo, and then while Zoe appeared to have agreed with Brad as to the definition of a 'Caravan', the pair of them couldn't have disagreed more when they came to consider Derek's purchases. What they could all understand, however, was that the club had a Planning Permission to put some caravans on its land, and as log cabins were *technically* caravans, the club could have either.

'Anyway,' said Derek, once his colleagues had stopped shuddering at the recollection of Brad's explanation. 'I reckoned that if caravans have to be made up of not more than two pieces, and there was one piece of each caravan at the bottom of the cliffs, then the other half of each caravan must still be at the top. Dunwich Hoo lost twelve caravans in that storm – six 'Windsors' and six 'Buckinghams'. I thought that if I bought the twelve half caravans that were still at the top of the cliff we'd be able to put six caravans back together from the pieces.'

'You complete fuck wit!' screamed Anna. 'Are you *honestly* telling us you thought there'd be a nice clean break down the middle of each caravan? Because if you *are* then you're even more stupid than I thought.'

Anna's outburst prompted a swift reprimand from Geoffrey about the use of inappropriate language regarding another member of the executive Committee, specifically that Derek could not, in all honesty, be regarded as more than an incomplete fuck wit, and a daft one at that. Having chastised Anna for not cursing Derek more thoroughly, Geoffrey offered the other Committee members the opportunity to curse their Treasurer before demanding that he explain himself further. Finally having recognised that he had no alternative but to come clean about the situation Derek told his colleagues as much as he knew.

'It turned out that some of those log cabins were relatively untouched, but some of the others were all but wrecked. So it seems that what was delivered here is about sixty per-cent of what we actually need to restore three 'Windsors' and three 'Buckinghams'.'

'So what do we do now?' asked Anna. 'Has anyone – other than Derek -got any bright ideas? Apart that is from hanging the stupid pillock from the nearest tree by his testicles. Or shall we just vote on that? Hands up all those in favour.'

'Oh dear,' said Derek as an average of approximately one point eight hands per Committee member were raised in the air.

***

Brad had been just as shocked as the Committee members to hear Derek's ludicrous explanation about the origin of the six piles of timber sitting just to one side of the club's car park. There had been some debate as to whether the Committee should tell the non-Committee winners – namely Brad, Leanne, Alice and Paul – about the situation just yet, but Geoffrey had convinced his Committee colleagues that honesty was the best policy, especially as they could in all honesty blame Derek. Brad was the first recipient of the news about the incomplete caravans

- after all it was he who had raised the issue with the Committee in the first place – and he reluctantly told Leanne what Geoffrey had told him. For Leanne the disappointment was akin to that she'd experienced with Brad in the early days, when he'd often delivered himself a happy ending way before she'd wanted him to, and well before she was ready. How things that changed in the intervening years, she thought to herself, regretting the fact she hadn't been more grateful at the time.

'So now what?' she asked Brad, although she really didn't expect him to be able to give any kind of answer.

'I don't know love,' Brad replied. 'I really don't know. Not unless you've got any bright ideas.'

Leanne thought about the problem, and how sharing a log cabin overlooking the lake with Brad might give the pair of them the quality time together Doctor Raja had prescribed in lieu of little blue pills, and how much Gwen might enjoy spending her final days in the surroundings she most loved.

'I might just have one,' she said after a couple of minutes. 'It's a long shot but I just might have an idea.'

# Chapter 21

Anna couldn't believe she was sitting in yet another committee meeting, although the truth of the matter was that technically she wasn't. The meeting was actually of the members of the Hidden Lake's executive Committee less one – that one being Derek. Although the incumbent Treasurer's absence didn't mean the meeting couldn't be considered quorate, the decision to exclude him from it – or even to advise him it was being held – could hardly be considered a shining example of democratic accountability.

'So what do we do about the situation?' said Geoffrey, to which Anna asked if he meant the piles of timber from which six log cabins were originally to have been constructed, or the twat whose fault it was the club currently found itself in such a mess.

'The cabins and their cost to the club,' replied Geoffrey. 'Although I can understand why we might want to consider the other.'

Despite the Treasurer's absence matters of finance were clearly on the Anna's mind as well as the Chairman's.

'Well has the club actually paid for them yet?' she asked. 'Or can we just refuse to pay for them on the basis they aren't what we ordered.'

'The problem with that,' replied Geoffrey. 'Is that a) we don't actually know what Derek did order, and b) I received a text alert from our bank advising that a transfer of funds had been made overnight. So the answer is - Yes, we are now the proud owners of six bloody great piles of wood.'

Geoffrey hadn't actually anticipated receiving that text alert, because he'd been expecting Derek to arrange to pay by cheque which the club could have stopped. The amount transferred had been the reduced sum Derek had said he'd 'negotiated' when the discrepancies in the shipment were first spotted, although the payee wasn't Dunwich Hoo Holdings but an unspecified business acquaintance of Derek's. The club may not have got quite what it was expecting out of Derek's shady deal, but the bottom line was that Derek had made damn sure he did.

*** 

Gwen couldn't remember the last time Leanne had spoken to her on the phone, let alone called her. It had come as a real shock when she realised that it was her daughter-in-law on the other end of the telephone line, that it had. Leanne had asked Gwen how she felt today, to which Gwen had replied that she didn't feel too good, but thank you for asking. It was George's fault really - Gwen had explained - which made Leanne wonder what the hell the old goat had been up to. So Leanne was relieved to learn that Gwen's current discomfort could be attributed to nothing more exotic than a visit to The Crown the previous evening.

'I told George I don't like foreign food,' Gwen explained. 'But he insisted that chicken tikka masala didn't really count as 'foreign', and that at a fiver for 'A ruby and a pint' - as he put it - you really couldn't go wrong. Well believe me dear, you can. I was up in the smallest room half the night, or so it seemed.'

Leanne realised that George had been correct in one of his assertions, namely that Britain's favourite 'Indian' dish actually originated in Glasgow, although Gwen remained firmly of the opinion that she wouldn't be trying it again anytime soon, because apart from shortbread and salmon she really didn't like Scottish food either.

'And how are you feeling now Gwen?' Leanne asked, partly out of compassion and partly because she needed to know if her mother-in-law was in a fit state to help her with a small problem.

'A lot better than I was last night dear, although I still daren't pass wind. I've put my biggest knickers on as a precaution, but even they aren't entirely bullet proof.'

Leanne was more than content to let that particular subject drop because - much like the Hidden Lake Club's executive Committee – there were some things about which she didn't like to pry, and because Gwen had already given her far too much information.

'So I shall be staying in today dear, just in case. I'm sure I can find something or other to occupy myself, although whatever it is I'll have to be within easy sprinting distance of the lavvy.'

*\*\**

The Hidden Lake Club's Committee members – less its incumbent Treasurer – had given up worrying about what to do with the log cabins and had reconvened their meeting to consider the sensitive issue of what to do about their absent colleague. Perhaps unsurprisingly it was Anna who made the first comment which Geoffrey felt sure would amount to the verbal equivalent of a stoning.

'He's a twat. A stupid twat and it's time we got rid of him. He's made a complete balls-up of the whole log cabin project, and it's time he went.'

'Perhaps we were partly to blame,' said Alison, at which suggestion Anna glared at the club's Secretary. 'Just as soon as we heard how little we might have to pay to get ourselves a log cabin we all wanted one. Didn't we? Yes, we did. We didn't stop to ask ourselves if it was too good a deal to be true, did we? No, we didn't. We were too worried that we might miss a bargain, weren't we? Yes, we were. In fact when you really come to think about it, we've no-one to blame but ourselves.'

'And Derek' replied Anna.

'And Derek, obviously.'

'The problem,' said Geoffrey. 'Is that without Derek we're never going to get the bits and pieces we need to put those cabins back together, even if we could afford them. But there's actually a much bigger problem.'

'And what's that?' asked Anna.

'Nobody in their right mind is going to be daft enough to take on the Treasurer's job, are they?'

The incomplete but quorate Committee paused for a moment to consider the situation, and realised that Geoffrey was absolutely right. Every time one of the Committee posts became vacant the club had one hell of a job trying to fill it. Potential candidates had been known to be bribed, threatened, and even - on one occasion – blackmailed, just to get them to sign up to the thankless task of becoming a member of the club's executive Committee. Automatic 'Gold' membership had never really been seen as sufficient compensation - perhaps until the right to buy a log cabin had arisen, but even that dream appeared to have now turned into a nightmare. The meeting appeared destined to go the way of most of the others, by going on all day and ending in disagreement, and it was well into the evening before an exhausted Geoffrey answered his mobile phone only to find one of the club's 'Silver' members on the line.

'Is that Mr Geoffrey Smith?' asked a female voice. 'Chairman of the Hidden Lake Sun Club.'

Geoffrey replied that indeed it was.

'Good,' said the caller. 'I am pleased to be able to tell you that I may have the answer to the problem of how to put your log cabins back together. Now, before we go any further I need to ask you some security questions. This call may also be recorded for training and security purposes.'

# Chapter 22

It was nearly a fortnight before Brad and Leanne were able to get down to the Hidden Lake Club again. They'd wanted to go down the previous weekend to start sorting out details for their log cabin, however Leanne had a long-standing commitment as Matron of Honour at an old girlfriend's wedding.

'Matron of Dishonour more like,' Brad grumbled as they sat in a queue of traffic just outside Grantham. 'What was it the last one died of?'

'Severe lacerations to the gonads caused as an indirect consequence of prolonged erectile dysfunction I believe dear,' said Leanne as she thumbed through a road map, hopelessly trying to find anything that said 'The North' next to it. 'But it's a relatively uncommon side effect, so I wouldn't worry too much about it if I were you. Not for the next couple of days anyway.'

'I don't see why she couldn't have found someone else to take your place. I mean, it's a bloody long way to Newcastle, and it's not as if you're bosom buddies.'

'It's important to her. She wants all her friends around her on her big day. I know I would.'

'She's had two big days already,' complained Brad. 'Is she going to get this one to love, honour and obey her like she did the others?'

'What do you mean?'

'Didn't the first one obey her by changing his Will to leave her a detached house in Cheshire shortly before he kicked the bucket?'

Leanne had to admit she didn't know the finer details of that Will, although she had thought it a bit odd that her friend's subsequent fiancé had insisted on a pre-nuptial agreement, only for the merry widow to call the wedding off shortly after, citing irreconcilable differences of opinion.

One thing Brad and Leanne did agree on was that this particular weekend away was more than a little inconvenient. In fact Brad had said that it was a right pain in the arse, although Leanne wasn't sure that particular comment didn't relate primarily to a set of roadworks just outside Doncaster. Be that as it may, both Brad and Leanne would have preferred to have spent the weekend at the Hidden Lake Club sorting out where to put their cabin, and protecting their chosen spot from the other winners who would also be looking for the perfect location for their own *des res*. In fact once Brad had vented his frustration about having to drive to Newcastle in the first place the discussion switched to their forthcoming project to build a log cabin, and of Gwen's part in solving a particularly tricky problem.

'I thought she'd be able to do it,' Leanne said as the reluctant travellers reached the outskirts of Newcastle. 'She's an amazing woman is your mother.'

Brad nodded his head and missed seeing a traffic light turn green. 'And the same to you chum,' he said, curling his middle finger and putting his right hand back on the steering wheel. 'Yes, you're right. She is an amazing woman. I'm so glad you two have buried the hatchet before either of you, well, buried a hatchet.'

Leanne agreed that she was happy the two women had patched up their differences after years of arguing, attempted poisoning, and alleging cocaine smuggling to name but three.

'Anyway, I can't believe how quickly she solved that puzzle about the pieces of the log cabins. I just told her what had happened at Dunwich Hoo, and how we'd only got part of them, and she went off and worked out how to make six smaller cabins from the bits we have got. I know there'll be a pile of pieces left over, but at least everybody who gets a cabin will now have one exactly the same. That should appeal to you because it's all very egalitarian, don't you think?'

'It is,' replied Brad. 'I was amazed when I spoke to Mother later that evening, and she told me she'd already solved the problem. As far as she was concerned it was just like one big jigsaw puzzle. In fact she'd even spoken to Geoffrey about it by the time I spoke to her.'

Leanne smiled. 'She told me that she'd be sitting in the lounge all day in case The Crown's chicken tikka masala took any further revenge, so I suppose it gave her something to do while she was waiting.'

Brad and Leanne's understanding of events was pretty much spot-on. Faced with a puzzle of how to try and make six log cabins out of six large piles of wood, Gwen had taken the list she'd written when the three lorries were unloaded, had cut a strip of paper for each piece of timber and had counted them out into one pile. Then she got a box of felt tipped pens and marked each strip of paper to indicate which size piece of timber

# Chapter 23

While Brad had been busy interrogating Zoe on the not-so-mysterious case of the six missing trees Leanne had been considering her options. Her current favourite - that of eloping with a dark, mysterious stranger with a significantly higher than average sex drive, and who was hung like a stallion wasn't really likely to happen, so Leanne reluctantly discounted it for the time being and returned to the subject of the log cabins. If others could manage to get their cabins in a lake-side setting then as far as Leanne was concerned so could she. There was a charming spot just a little further along the edge of the lake that particularly appealed to her, particularly as it offered lovely views across the lake to some small man-made islands beyond. Unfortunately those lovely views were currently blocked by a large willow, and the exact location Leanne had selected for her cabin was currently occupied by a large alder. Of course, if the others could arrange for a couple of trees to be removed then Leanne felt quite sure that she could too. There was no point referring the matter to Brad, because he'd just witter on endlessly about fucking Tree Preservation Orders and somebody at the club getting their arse kicked if the authorities ever found out. But exactly who to see about getting the offending trees removed? Leanne considered the situation for a couple of minutes. Perhaps she'd have a quiet word with Alice and Paul? After all, they weren't on the executive Committee so they shouldn't have any rights or privileges that she and Brad, as 'Gold' members didn't also have. As it turned out Leanne didn't need to seek help from Alice and Paul because before she had the opportunity to speak to them Brad returned. Just as Leanne had predicted her husband started to rabbit on about how the trees had been removed *illegally*, and how it was all very *serious*, and how the guilty party could get their backside kicked very hard if the Council ever found them out. From Leanne's perspective, however, Brad had provided just the information she needed to get the chainsaws primed.

'Can you believe it?' Brad had moaned. 'Zoe's only gone and used a provision relating to urgent works to trees on the basis of them being either 'dead, dying or dangerous' as an excuse to get them removed. She reckons they either had honey fungus, or.. er, where are you going?'

Leanne didn't bother to reply to her husband's question although she did have one of her own to pose to Alice and Paul, although it was no longer to whom should she speak.

***

'Just over there,' came the reply when Leanne asked the proud owners of a cabin overlooking the lake where she could find Zoe. 'Near to where you were standing earlier.'

Leanne walked back to the spot where she'd been considering she'd get a gorgeous view over the lake if only a pesky tree or two were removed. Just as Alice had said she would Leanne found Zoe.

'Those two trees might need to come out Zoe,' Leanne said as she pointed to the willow and alder in turn. 'What's wrong with them do you think? Might they be suffering from some nasty, incurable tree disease, or might they be dangerous perhaps? The don't look at all well to me.'

'There's nothing wrong with them,' replied Zoe. 'They're fine, healthy specimens as far as I can see.'

Leanne shook her head. 'No, you don't understand. Those two trees need to come out. So I'll ask you again. What's wrong with those trees Zoe?'

'Nothing,' replied Zoe. 'I've just told you. Your Brad's very concerned about the removal of healthy trees, so I'd hate to think I'd been complicit in the destruction of such fine, healthy specimens. After all, the penalties for removal without consent are severe.'

Despite Zoe's refusal to diagnose either of the tees with a terminal condition, Leanne was determined not to dance to Zoe's tune. She briefly contemplated seeing if she could find the pointed stick she'd once used to demonstrate how to dispose of an unwanted mother-in-law, but reckoned the chances of finding it would be pretty slim, even assuming that Brad hadn't chucked it on his damn bonfire. However, if she did find the stick or something of a similar size and weight Leanne was sure she could be highly persuasive and convince Zoe that the trees requiring removal were actually in a poor state of health, because if they weren't Zoe very soon would be.

Unfortunately none of the woodland debris appeared to be suitable for the purpose Leanne had in mind, so despite the threat of severe internal injury providing a compelling argument in favour of agreeing with her suggestion, Leanne eventually decided on an alternative course of action. Making her way further into the woods Leanne eventually found what he was looking for. It was sticking out from one side of a large birch tree, was mottled yellow-brown on one side and a creamy white on the other, and had a peculiar, earthy smell. Exactly what sort of fungus this was Leanne had absolutely no idea, but that didn't matter. Taking a paper tissue from her pocket – after all, some of these things can be deadly poisonous – Leanne broke off a chunk of the fungus and carefully wrapped it up.

Of all the Committee members she could have tried to find Derek was by far the best choice, and Leanne was delighted to find him busily working on his own log cabin.

'There's a willow and an alder over there that need taking out Derek,' Leanne said as she pointed towards the desired site for her own log cabin. 'Really nasty case of honey fungus. Here, have a look.'

Leanne carefully unwrapped the tissue containing her sample of the unknown fungus, and showed it to the club's errant Treasurer.

'Very badly infected I'm afraid. The trees you had to remove had honey fungus too, didn't they?'

Derek nodded his head and inspected the contents of Leanne's tissue. Zoe had told him all about honey fungus. How there was no treatment and no cure, and how the only way to deal with diseased specimens was to remove them as quickly as possible and burn them. In fact the closest thing Derek had actually seen to honey fungus was the few wispy strands of ginger hair that had sprouted from his ex-wife when her HRT went slightly awry.

'Yes, they had to be removed,' replied Derek, in a response which could have applied equally to the growth on his ex-wife's chest.

'I'll get Bill to get the chainsaw busy during the week. How about Tuesday?'

Leanne replied that any day of the week would be just fine with her, and that was because she knew that Zoe worked Mondays-Fridays, although she didn't tell Derek as much. So that was the removal of the offending trees dealt with, now all Leanne had to arrange was for disposal of the evidence.

'By the way Derek, did you ever get your gas heating fixed, or are you still relying on that old wood burner? If I were you I'd think about getting some logs in ready for next winter, just in case. Well, can you believe it? I've just thought of something. You know those two trees we were just talking about?'

Derek replied that he had got his heating sorted out, just, but that Leanne was quite right and that he should think about next winter, and that he should arrange to get some logs in. What Derek didn't say was that he'd already got more than enough timber to meet his needs for at least the next three winters, and was now offering it around his local at £50 a trailer load.

Leanne smiled. It had been a good afternoon's work. She'd staked a claim for her log cabin down by the lakeside, had arranged for the removal of the two 'dying' trees, and even arranged for disposal of the evidence —sorry, contaminated timber. It was all very Wild West, and all very exciting. All she needed to do now was to figure out exactly how she was going to placate Brad when he went ape-shit about what she'd been up to.

\*\*\*

Leanne hadn't misjudged her husband's reaction to her endeavours when she eventually told him what was going to happen. There was no point trying to lie to him by telling him that Zoe had agreed to it, because he'd only go and talk to the damn woman. No, better by far to tell the truth, but at the same time to be economic with it and use her womanly charms concurrently.

'You've done *what*?' demanded Brad when Leanne broached the subject of the location of their log cabin. 'Are you telling me that you've gone and got Zoe to agree to take out two more trees?'

'No darling, I'm telling you that I've managed to get us a lake-side spot for our cabin - which is wonderful news, isn't it?'

Despite Leanne's attempt at playing the spin-doctor Brad wasn't to be put off-course.

'But that's going to mean two more trees have got to come out, doesn't it?'

'Well, sort of.'

'Never mind "Sort of." It that yes or no?'

'Well, I er, - Look Brad, if the others can have lake-side cabins we should be able to as well.'

'So that's a 'Yes' then, is it?'

'Well, if you put it that way I suppose.'

Brad shut his eyes and put his head in his hands, and Leanne began to realise that all this business about Tree Preservation Orders really did matter to him. Perhaps more worryingly from her perspective, she realised that Brad's worrying about the loss of some damn timber wouldn't do anything to help him get the relaxation Doctor Raja had prescribed to help him get his own personal wood back. It was time for Leanne to play her Ace, and the Ace was called Gwen.

'I *know* I really shouldn't have done it sweetheart,' Leanne cooed as she put her index finger to her lips, pouted and gave Brad her best 'Little Girl Lost' look that used to remove the creases from Brad's underwear in no time at all. 'But I was only thinking of you and me, and Gwen and George.'

'Mother and Father?'

'Yes sweetheart. I thought it might be nice if we were to – maybe - let them use the cabin for a few days, when the time comes. Or maybe a couple of weeks or so. After all, Gwen said she wants to spend her final days overlooking the lake. What do you think darling?'

Brad hadn't expected such an act of generosity from Leanne towards his parents, but he could see it was offered from the heart, and was grateful for that.

'I'd been thinking exactly the same thing actually,' he said. 'In fact there's not a lot of point us moving into the cabin yet, is there? We don't know how much time Mother has left, so perhaps we should just get the cabin up, fit it out as best we can to make it all nice and comfy, and let the pair of them use it until - Well until. How's that with you?'

Brad's idea wasn't *quite* what Leanne had in mind, particularly as there didn't appear to be a satisfactory definition of 'until', but she could see the sense in what he was proposing. By the time the pair of them had got their log cabin completed and furnished who knows how much of the summer would remain, or how much time Gwen would have left to enjoy it? But more importantly, perhaps, agreeing to Brad's suggestion would distract him from the minor matter of two trees being felled in a couple of days' time, and of her complicity in it.

'We'll have to get it up first,' said Brad, to which Leanne looked at him quizzically.

'The log cabin. We'll have to get the log cabin up before we tell Mother and Father about our proposals.'

'Oh, er, yes. For a minute there I thought you meant something else.'

Leanne turned away from her husband and muttered to herself.

'It's a bloody good job that's what you did mean otherwise the poor old bugger would probably be long gone by then.'

# Chapter 24

Derek had been good to his word, and by the time Brad and Leanne returned to the Hidden Lake Club the following weekend the offending alder and willow had been removed, and even the stumps ground out. Leanne made a mental note to get Bill a nice bottle of Pinot Grigio as a small token of appreciation for his efforts, and Brad made a mental note to avoid telling anyone that he'd known anything of the real reason why the two trees had been removed.

By late Saturday afternoon the cabin's ground works were largely complete, and by the end of Sunday a solid base had been completed ready for the cabin to be built over it. Now it was just a case of putting the thing together from the piles of logs, planks and other bit and pieces that were currently sitting under a large tarpaulin just behind their proposed final resting place. Brad and Leanne had both booked a couple of days' annual leave from work to try and get their cabin built, and as it was only a short drive from home to the Hidden Lake Club they were reasonably confident they'd have the thing largely complete by Tuesday evening. They certainly didn't feel they were being over-optimistic, particularly as Alice and Paul had almost completed their cabin, and were happy for Brad and Leanne to use it as a template. Working around the cabin, one side at a time, Brad and Leanne would identify the size of the next piece of timber they needed by looking at Alice and Paul's cabin, and then selecting the correct type from the pile available. Round and round the cabin they went. First a short piece at the front – where the door would be going – then one much longer piece to go along the left hand side. Then a piece of timber for the rear, and then another longer piece for the right hand side. Finally, another short piece of timber - to go next to the other side of the door - before starting the whole process all over again. Brad and Leanne had to retrace their steps at one point, when Leanne belatedly decided she wanted one of the cabin's windows on the left-hand side rather than on the right where Alice and Paul had put theirs, but otherwise the job was reasonably straightforward. In fact it wasn't until works had progressed as far as the front door that things got more complicated, and unfortunately the D-I-Y instruction sheet Tina and Jeffrey had downloaded from Meritorious Sheds didn't help much.

'It's for a different model, surely?' Brad complained as he looked at the printed A4 sheets on which the assembly instructions were written. 'It says *'Fit longitudinal timber B101 over cross-brace BX10.'* Have we got a BX10?'

'I'm fucked if I know,' came the reply, and Brad rightly concluded that his wife had no idea what a BX10 cross-brace looked like, let alone whether or not they had one to fit to longitudinal timber B101.

'Then it says *'Fit inner transom C5 over end plate and secure in place using 3 off M10 x 100.'* Have we got 3 off M10 x 100 Leanne?'

Leanne replied exactly as she had regarding the BX10 cross-brace, and its relationship with longitudinal timber B101.

'This isn't easy you know Leanne.'

Leanne sighed. 'Look Brad, I'm absolutely bloody knackered, and I've had enough. Shall we call it a day?'

'Let's just get this bit done shall we? That'll be a good place to stop. Now, it says here '*Be sure to screw firmly from rear.*' What do you make of that?'

Leanne replied that she didn't give a toss whether Brad screwed from the f'ing front or from the f'ing rear, just as long as he made some kind of f'ing effort now and again. Because if he didn't Leanne promised him that she'd find another f'ing use for his new f'ing battery-powered multi-purpose, oscillating f'ing tool and it wouldn't be one listed on the f'ing instruction manual either. What was more, it was a damn good job that the said f'ing multi-purpose tool had come with two f'ing high-power, quick charge f'ing batteries, because the way she was feeling right now she'd still be going after more than one twenty-minute recharge cycle.

Brad took Leanne's less than subtle hint, and agreed they'd had more than enough for one day, so he started to pack his tools away. He hoped Leanne hadn't been serious when she said what she would do with his new multi-purpose tool if he failed to attempt to perform from one side or the other, because the limited twenty-four month warranty sure as hell didn't cover the activity she'd had in mind. More worryingly, if Leanne did manage to bugger up the mechanics in her enthusiasm he'd have one hell of a job explaining to the Customer Services girl at B&Q just how on earth he'd managed to get it broken in the first place.

# Chapter 25

The following day Brad and Leanne returned to the vexed question of longitudinal timbers, cross-braces, transoms and the like. In fact they soon managed to solve the problems which had appeared intractable the previous evening, their apparent complexity partly attributable to the fact that Brad had turned two pages of the instruction sheets over at once, and partly because those instructions were for a different model of cabin entirely. By lunchtime the pair had most of the front porch assembled and little remained to be done apart from fitting some minor bits and pieces and accessories such as the door, windows and part of the roof. Brad was just fixing what he'd thought the previous day was inner transom C5 in place when something crossed his mind.

'I suppose we'll have to clear it with the Committee.'

'Clear what with the Committee?' replied Leanne.

'Letting Mother and Father use our cabin for the rest of the season.'

'It's got bugger all to do with them surely? It's our cabin.'

Although Brad would have preferred to simply let Gwen and George use the log cabin in lieu of him and Leanne and said nothing to the Committee, he remembered that one of the conditions attached to its purchase was that the cabin was to be used solely by its owners.

'Yes it's our cabin, but there were string attached to its occupation if you remember. One of those conditions of sale was that each cabin is to be occupied by its owners, with occupation by any other person - or persons - incurring a camping fee at the club's normal daily rate.'

'You mean we'd have to pay extra to allow your mother and father to use it?'

'Well under normal circumstances somebody would, but I'm sure if we have a word with the Committee they'll use their discretion. After all, they're aware of the situation, and I'm sure they'd all like Mother to be able to spend her final days in her favourite spot. We'll just have to appeal to their better side, that's all.'

'Well I'm not sure that Anna's got one, and I'm bloody sure Derek hasn't.'

Brad sighed as he realised that one apparently small request might well involve the entire Committee in an interminable debate. 'Perhaps I'll have a quiet word with Geoffrey,' he said. 'He's a good, no-nonsense sort of chap. Yes, I'll have a quiet word with him.'

Brad's musings on the best way to gain the Committee's blessing for Gwen and George to occupy the cabin were brought to an abrupt halt as a chainsaw was ripped into life not fifty yards from where he was standing, and any thoughts other than the fate of yet another tree were lost completely as the trunk of a slender birch came crashing to the ground. The demise of the tree not being due to an act of God, Brad decided to go and find out exactly why it had received a death sentence. He didn't have to look very hard before he found Bill toting a smoking chainsaw.

'Was that one dead, dying or dangerous Bill?' Brad shouted just as soon as the chainsaw had been turned off.

'Dying,' came the reply.

'Honey fungus?'

'Yes, according to Zoe. How did you know anyway?'

'Just a hunch,' muttered Brad, wondering exactly why that particular tree needed to be removed other than to improve the view from somebody's log cabin. Whatever the reason Brad left Leanne to try and work out which way around she wanted their cabin's windows to open, and wandered across to where the birch tree had once stood. Bill was just about to start up his chainsaw again ready to cut the trunk of the birch tree into convenient, wood-burner sized pieces when he noticed Brad approaching.

'Shame it had to come down, but on the plus side it'll make it easier to get the drive laid.'

'Drive? What drive?'

'The driveway from the car park to the cabins. Didn't you know? They want me to lay a drive from the car park so that the cabin's owners don't have so far to carry their bits and pieces when they come to stay. That'll be a plus for you, what with your cabin being where it is.'

'So you're telling me there's going to be a driveway through the *woods*?'

'Yeah, although some of it'll be a rough track because we can't afford to do it all in tarmac at the moment. There's going to be a conduit with a power cable under it too, in case the owners decide they want to have electricity in their cabins. Mind you they'll have to pay for it.'

Brad shook his head in disbelief at what he was hearing.

'One of the joys of this place is its beautiful, natural surroundings. We seem to be determined to destroy the very character of the place we all treasure.'

'You'll have to take that up with the Committee Brad, it's nothing to do with me. I'm just following instructions.'

Brad muttered something about Nuremburg and people just obeying orders, but unfortunately Bill didn't hear a word of it as he'd put his ear protectors back on, and was furiously pulling at the chainsaw's starter cord. The brief conversation was clearly at an end, and Bill clearly didn't wish to be interrogated further, so Brad waved goodbye and turned away ready to walk back to his log cabin. He'd only walked a couple of yards before he saw Geoffrey walking in the direction of the clubhouse, so Brad made a minor deviation to his route and was soon walking shoulder to shoulder with the club's Chairman.

'Can I have a quick word Geoffrey?' Brad asked as soon as he was within earshot, and at a volume which made allowance for Geoffrey not having his hearing aid switched on.

'And what quick word would that be Brad? 'No' is a quick word, and particularly suitable if it involves spending any of the club's money.'

'Very funny. I need to have a word with you about Mother and Father.'

Geoffrey stopped walking and fiddled with his left ear, suggesting to Brad that he had been correct in his assumption about Geoffrey's hearing aid.

'What about them?'

'Well, because of Mother's illness Leanne and I were – are – proposing to let them use our log cabin until she's no longer with us - That's to say she's at home, or is in a home, or is – well – I think you understand.'

Geoffrey nodded, confirming that he did understand, although he didn't ask any questions as he really didn't like to pry.

'Do you see any problems with that?'

Geoffrey shook his head, suggesting to Brad that he didn't see any problems, although as soon as Geoffrey spoke it was clear to Brad that he should have waited before coming to any conclusions.

'I think they're both 'Silver' members, so provided they pay the camping fee at the normal daily rate I don't see any problems at all.'

'Ah,' replied Brad. 'I was rather hoping we could come to some alternative arrangement.'

'Such as?'

'Well, Leanne and I are both 'Gold' members so we've already paid for unlimited camping rights for the summer season. We were thinking that *perhaps* Mother and Father could use those rights instead of us? After all, we're the same family, and we've both got the same surname. So the site would still be allocated to a Mr and Mrs Dixon, it's just that it would be G & G Dixon instead of B & L. What do you think? I know it's not exactly following the rules, but bearing in mind the circumstances do you think the club could make an exception?'

Geoffrey breathed in deeply and as he did so he made a whistling noise between his teeth, similar to that plumbers and motor mechanics make when they are about to tell you that something's well and truly knackered, and is going to be horribly expensive to repair.

'Well I'm not sure we could agree to that. Personally I'd be happy to, you understand, but I'm not sure my Committee colleagues would all be too happy. You see Brad, the problem is that the club is desperately short of funds, and allowing *you* a concession could open the flood gates to all sorts of other exceptions. I know at least one other family who would like to sub-let their cabin out during the school holidays. And I'm also aware of a member who appears rather keen on sharing his cabin with a 'Bronze' member for *gratis* from time to time, although to be honest I'm not sure if the lady in question is actually aware of his intentions. Either way, there's a vast number of potential 'special circumstances' that could arise, all of which could reduce the club's income at a time of considerable need.'

'Oh,' replied Brad, only for Geoffrey to set off on a further justification of his decision before Brad had a chance to put forward any further proposals.

'And of course - as you said yourself - you and Leanne are 'Gold' members with unlimited camping rights. Now, what would happen if the pair of you wanted to camp for a few nights and George and Gwen were occupying that log cabin? There'd be an extra fee to pay, wouldn't there? And how much would that fee be? The answer is we just don't know. You see Brad, none of this has been thought through yet. Maybe in a year or so we'll have these various scenarios all worked out and a proper price list drawn up, but in the meantime if I give you special dispensation it could lead to all manner of accusations of impropriety, and in my position I simply cannot risk that.'

'Despite my mother's condition?'

Geoffrey sighed and it was quite obvious that he'd overlooked Gwen's illness when denying Brad any special deals.

'Oh dear, yes. I do understand. Um..'

There was a slight pause while Geoffrey tried to work out how he could extract himself from the quagmire and potential accusations of being a tight bastard.

'I'll tell you what Brad,' he eventually said. 'Here's what I can do..'

# Chapter 26

Brad and Leanne didn't want to waste any time before letting George and Gwen know about their decision to let them use the log cabin, so instead of driving straight home they made a slight diversion to George and Gwen's bungalow confident that they'd be at home. The doorbell had just finished playing a synthesised version of 'Colonel Bogey' when Brad heard his father's voice through the letterbox.

'Whatever it is you're selling we don't want it, so bugger off.'

'It's only us Father.'

'Why didn't you say so? – Stay there and I'll let you in.'

Apart from shouting through the letterbox Brad wasn't quite sure how he could have let his father know it was his son and daughter in law, and not some ne'er-do-well intent on relieving a pair of pensioners of their hard-earned savings, but it didn't really matter. Instead, Brad waited as George unlocked a bolt at the top of the door, then one at the bottom, followed by a third bolt next to the latch. Finally he undid a chain.

'You could have just come around the back you know,' George said as he opened one half of a pair of wooden doors. 'It's always open.'

Brad and Leanne wiped their shoes on a coarse bristle doormat emblazoned with the words 'Please Remove Your Clothes' and which deposited as much dirt on the carpet underneath as it caught within its bristles. Their shoes relieved of any loose debris and their bodies defying the doormat's instruction by remaining fully clothed, Brad and Leanne entered George and Gwen's entrance hall.

'Oh hello dear,' said Gwen, as she emerged from the smallest room. 'This is a nice surprise.'

'We've got something important we want to tell you,' said Leanne. 'And we didn't want to wait until tomorrow.'

'Oh that's *wonderful* news darling,' replied Gwen, and she flung her arms around her daughter-in-law.

'We haven't told you what it is yet Mother,' Brad said just as his father decided now was the time to shake his son's hand. But Gwen had already decided what the announcement was going to be.

'You're pregnant aren't you Leanne? Oh, that is such good news. But tell me, under the circumstances that you and my genitally dysfunctional son find yourselves, how do they do it these days? It is still with a length of rubber tubing and a pipette, or have they gone all digital and multi-media?'

'Well unless there's been some miraculous change in his condition it'd have to be one or other,' said George as he pointed to Brad's crotch. 'So, did they attach a vacuum pump to you, or did the pair of you end up using a donor?'

'I'm not pregnant,' replied Leanne, rather firmly and just before Brad was going to demand his father drop the subject immediately.

'Are you sure dear?' replied Gwen. 'I was sure you'd been carrying a few extra pounds these last few weeks.'

Leanne had to grit her teeth but somehow managed to retain her composure.

'I'm absolutely sure Gwen.'

'Not just a little tiny bit?'

'No Gwen sweetheart, I'm not even a little bit pregnant. Your dear son hasn't had the necessary apparatus in a functional condition to put me in that state for some time now. So no, I'm not pregnant, believe me. I've tried everything I know to get his thing moving in an upward direction but nothing has had the slightest effect.'

'Well why don't we have a look on the Interweb dear,' suggested Gwen as she sat herself down in an armchair. 'George, kick up the computer and we'll see what we can find.'

'No,' replied Brad. 'That's not a good idea. You've no idea what you might find out there, and anyway that's not why we're here. We actually wanted to let you know about our log cabin..'

Brad was about to break the good news to his parents, but didn't get a chance because Leanne beat him to it.

'We've decided, Brad and I - well it was *my* idea really, but we both agreed – to let you both use our log cabin for as long as you need it.' Leanne took hold of her mother-in-law's hand and held it tightly. 'You always said you wanted to spend your final days overlooking the lake, next to the spot where your lovely kingfisher perches, didn't you? And now you shall.'

For once in her life Gwen seemed to be lost for words, and it was a minute or so before she spoke.

'I don't know what to say dear. That's very kind of you, isn't it George?'

George nodded his agreement that he also thought it was very kind.

'The cabin's almost ready to move into,' said Leanne. 'We've cleared everything with the Committee, or at least the ones who actually matter, so you just need to sort out what bits and pieces you need to make it homely, and then we'll help you move in. Brad's got a few odds and ends to sort out - including his own odd end, but that's another story altogether.'

Gwen still appeared lost for words, and when she did speak it was only to reiterate her previous thoughts.

'That's so kind of you both. I really don't know what to say.'

'There's no need to say anything,' replied Leanne. 'Just get together whatever you'll need for a long weekend away to start with, and then we'll think about what else you might need for a longer stay.'

Gwen nodded her head, then got up from her armchair and threw her arms around Leanne, giving her daughter-in-law an almighty bear hug that almost winded the pair of them.

'So how much to do we owe you then?' asked George. 'The club must be making some charge for us using the cabin instead of you. They wouldn't miss out on a trick like that, no way. That Derek's a tight bastard and Geoffrey's no fool.'

'Nothing,' replied Brad, wondering if perhaps he might have got a better deal by negotiating with the fool Derek rather than the tight bastard Geoffrey. 'We've done a deal with the Committee, so you can call it a present from the pair of us.'

'No dear, we insist,' said Gwen, just as soon as she'd released Leanne from her clutches. 'You've done so much for us already it's only fair that we pay.'

'She's right you know,' added George.

'I'll tell you what,' said Leanne. 'How about you and George pay the daily camping fee as if you were staying in a tent rather than a log cabin? How does that sound?'

'Sounds like a deal to me,' replied George.

Gwen agreed with George that they'd pay the daily camping fee for a tent rather than a log cabin, which made a total of three of the Dixon family in favour to one against. The one against – namely Brad – was perfectly content that Gwen and George pay something if they really wanted to, but wasn't so happy that his wife appeared to have palmed his parents off with exactly the same deal Geoffrey had given him. That 'deal' would leave his parents no better off than if they'd negotiated with the Committee themselves. That - as he saw it - was no present, and it wasn't really fair that Leanne had suggested it was. Still - as Gwen had said earlier - he and Leanne had done a lot for the pair of them recently, so taking everything into account Brad felt he could still justifiably claim a Boy Scout's 'Helping Elderly Parents' badge.

# Chapter 27

Over the next few days Brad and Leanne helped George and Gwen get the log cabin ready for occupation. Brad finished off some minor construction work to the cabin itself, while Leanne kept busy ferrying her in-laws back and forth between their bungalow, the Hidden Lake Club, and their nearest leisure and camping shop. Eventually the cabin was complete and ready for George and Gwen to move into, and had all the facilities needed for a comfortable, if fairly basic, few days away from home. None of the log cabins had running water, mains power or drainage – not yet anyway, although Brad was in little doubt that they would eventually, even if it did result in another lengthy session for Bill's with his damned chainsaw. To overcome these minor inconveniences Brad installed a small domestic cold water tank on a raised platform at the rear of the cabin which could be filled as required from one of the nearby standpipes. The tank was then connected via a plastic pipe to a sink in the cabin, so that it could supply cold water for rinsing plates, washing hands, and the like, with the waste water running to a soakaway outside the cabin. Keen to demonstrate his ecological credentials, Brad fitted two solar panels to the roof of the cabin, partly as a longer-term investment for when he and Leanne eventually moved in, and partly as a silent eco-protest at the slow destruction of the club's native woodlands. The solar panels only supplied twelve volts, but connected to a large car battery they were more than sufficient to power lighting, George's electric razor and Gwen's portable television. Finally, Brad constructed a studwork partition with a door to form a small cubicle, despite being only a three minute walk from the club's shower block. Octogenarians, George had explained, could not realistically be expected to go all night without getting up for a pee, and be buggered if he or Gwen were going to squat in the woods at three o' clock in the morning should nature place any calls.

'Just as long as it's big enough to sit down in,' George replied when Brad asked him how big the cubicle should be. 'And get up again, but to be on the safe side can you fit a couple of grab handles on the walls while you're at it?'

Brad did as George asked, and also fitted a small wash-hand basin which he plumbed into the cabin's rudimentary cold water system. George was right of course, it would be bloody inconvenient wandering around the woods at night with a torch in one hand and a roll of toilet paper in the other, especially if it was raining. Alright, so bears didn't have a problem with it, but on the other hand bears don't get back to their dens only to find the toilet roll's got soaked and has swollen up to ten times its normal size. No, a portable lavvy was a sound investment and a thoroughly worthwhile addition to the cabin's inventory, provided that it was Leanne's job to clean and empty it.

*** 

To Brad's surprise it took a total of four journeys to transport all the bits and pieces George and Gwen's thought they might need from their bungalow to the log cabin, by which time he was beginning to understand the desirability of having an access driveway from the club's car park. Brad almost joked with his parents that they weren't making a permanent move, but then realised the possibility of it being just that for Gwen, and managed to avoid saying anything which might upset either of them. As far as the actual move was concerned it would have helped if George had stipulated that the new self-assembly double bed he'd ordered be delivered to the Hidden Lake Club and not his home address but, as he pointed out when Brad queried it, he couldn't be sure when the cabin would be ready. At fifty per-cent off that weekend the new bed was a bargain he really didn't want to miss. Despite two of the four trips to the club being dedicated to transporting pieces of the new bed Brad managed to retain a sense of humour, joking that at fifty per-cent off George could have bought two for the price of one, effectively getting himself another BOGOF deal.

'By the way Father,' Brad said as he finished loading timber slats into the car through its side passenger window. 'Did you ever hear anything from any of those companies about your claim that they'd used the idea of BOGOF promotions without your consent?'

'Bollocks did I,' complained George. 'The miserable bastards didn't even cover the postage. We got a couple of letters thanking us for our 'communication' and a few money-off coupons for stuff we don't use, or which we can get cheaper elsewhere, but other than that it was a complete waste of time. I still use the computer now and then, and I've got dozens of Eastern European women who say they want to meet me for some 'no-strings attached' fun. One of them only lives two miles down the road according to her website.'

'I'd stay well clear of the lot of them if I were you,' replied Brad. 'I certainly would, that's for sure.'

'Well given your particular circumstances you would, wouldn't you? The last thing you'd want is the raven-haired, 21 year-old Natalya, originally from Smolensk – 36, 24, 36 – hopelessly rummaging around in your boxer shorts only to find her womanly charms have been completely wasted on you. I mean, how embarrassing would that be?'

'It wouldn't be the slightest bit embarrassing because I'm never going to get into that situation,' replied Brad.

'Not embarrassing for you, you chump, for her. Can you imagine how she'd feel? She'd be far better off sticking to an older, more reliable man with a proven track record.' George nudged his son in the ribs. 'So have a quiet word with your mother for me will you the next time you get a chance? She still won't let me go and find out what the score is.'

Brad had no hesitation in telling his father that he'd do no such thing, because as far as Brad was concerned George's days of 'no-strings attached' fun should have ended the last time he paid his bill at Mr Patel's Penang Passion parlour.

*** 

The final trip to the cabin was more of a ceremonial affair rather than anything else. Gwen had a few last bits and pieces she wanted to take with her, but otherwise Brad and Leanne's car was devoid of George and Gwen's personal possessions, and the boot contained only what Leanne had decided she and Brad needed for a day at the club. The idea was that George and Gwen would stay overnight as the weather forecast was set fair, and that Brad and Leanne would return the following day to take George and Gwen back home on the Sunday evening.

When they arrived at their log cabin Brad was delighted to see that their friends had put up a large banner across the front of the cabin with the words 'Welcome Gwen and George' on it, and had tied a ribbon across the door. Brad gave his mother a pair of scissors and she cut the ribbon in two, to applause from all her friends who had gathered to wish the couple well. Alison and Steve jokingly suggested that George should carry Gwen over the threshold, however George declined to do so on the basis that his back wasn't what it used to be, although fortunately he didn't go into the reasons why.

Everything inside the cabin was ready, so Brad and Leanne waited until George and Gwen had got themselves settled in, and then got ready to go home. It was only when they were half-way back to their house that a thought crossed Leanne's mind, and it related to something that both she and Brad had completely overlooked despite Geoffrey raising it when he was trawling up excuses why he couldn't allow George and Gwen to stay in the log cabin for free.

'Brad,' she said. 'Now that George and Gwen have got our site, where are we going to camp?'

It might have been prudent for Leanne to wait until they weren't sitting at a red traffic light before asking that question, because Brad's powers of concentration were immediately diverted away from the traffic lights and onto the matter of a camping pitch. In fact his mind was still solely occupied with that thought when the drivers of the two cars behind him decided they'd had enough of the prat still sitting stationery in front of them at a green light, and let him know as much with their horns.

'To be honest I hadn't thought of that,' replied Brad once the car was moving again, and he'd reassured himself that Leanne had sought to take the credit for letting George and

Gwen use the log cabin. 'They'll find us something, I'm sure they will.'

'Well I bloody well hope they do, because it'll be a miserable summer if we have to go back home every evening and miss out on camping overnight.'

'You mean we'll miss out on all the gossip, don't you?'

'Possibly that as well.'

'I thought as much. Alright, I'll have a word with one of the Committee when we go back to pick Mother and Father up tomorrow. I'm sure there's a camping pitch available somewhere on the site.' Brad paused momentarily and then sighed. 'After all, now they've cut down so many trees there must be a lot more pitches available.'

***

As it turned out Derek wasn't any more sympathetic to Brad and Leanne's situation than Geoffrey had been regarding a reduced fee for the Dixon seniors to use the juniors' log cabin. He'd been the first Committee member that Brad had set eyes on that day, and Brad had no reason to suspect that Derek would be any less sympathetic to his plight than any of the others.

'We haven't got any spare pitches left,' Derek said when Brad told him of their predicament, and asked where they could pitch their tent for the remainder of the season.

'You must have *loads* of spare pitches, surely?' said Brad. 'Now half the trees have gone. Look, we've paid for 'Gold' membership and Mother and Father are also paying the club to use our cabin, so you're really taking money from us on false pretences if we can't camp here.'

'The problem is that those log cabins have turned out to be hugely desirable summer residences. As a result the vast majority of the club's members have put their names down for one, and now we've got a waiting list as long as your right arm. That gives us a problem on several counts including where the hell we'd put them, but mainly it's a problem because we can't get any more like the ones we already have. This isn't finalised yet so I'm telling you in confidence, but we're proposing a second row behind the existing cabins, although that would mean..'

'Another load of trees would have to come down.'

'Well, yes, but I was going to say that it would probably mean we'd end up with a load of static caravans rather than log cabins, but under English planning law they're the same thing, or so you once spend ages trying to convince us.'

Brad winced at the thought of a row of static caravans sitting behind the existing log cabins. He was in no doubt that Zoe had already advised the Committee that, in her opinion, Planning Permission wouldn't be required, and had little doubt that any trees in the way would mysteriously succumb to honey fungus in the few weeks following the Committee's final decision. Trees had already been lost at an alarming rate, and the wooded grounds that made the club such a wonderfully tranquil spot in which to relax would soon start to resemble a prairie with a fence around the outside, and a trailer park shoved in the middle of it.

'Well that doesn't really help us, does it?' Brad said once the apocalyptic vision of the club's last tree being felled had cleared from his mind sufficiently for him to speak. 'We've paid for unlimited camping, and you're saying we can't have it. The least you can do is give us a refund.'

Strangely the idea of giving a refund prompted Derek to conjure up an alternative site, although it wasn't one Brad would have chosen, even if he'd known about it.

'Well, there's an old camping site on the way down to the ditch you could probably use.'

Brad didn't know where Derek meant, so he asked for further directions to which Derek waved his arms around and pointed towards the lavatories.

'You go down past the shower block and the area where the septic tank is – Leanne will know where I mean – and then before you get down to the ditch you'll see the pitch on the left hand side. It might be a bit overgrown now, and it hasn't been used for years. That track used to be known as Shite Alley, and we used to put some of the visitors from the Greenlands club nearby from time to time if it was dry. You could use that I suppose.'

Although Brad was relieved to hear that an alternative site appeared to be available, the street naming didn't appear as if it had been carried out by the local Council.

'Did I hear you call it 'Shite Alley'?'

'Don't worry about that. It's fine now the septic tank's sorted out. You'll be upwind of it anyway because the weather's coming in from the west this week. That lot from Greenlands were always a bit too fussy for my liking.'

# Chapter 28

It took Brad and Leanne most of the morning to clear the site for their tent, and by the time they'd finished there was a pile of bracken, grass and weeds over three feet high sitting in the middle of the track formerly known as 'Shite Alley'. Unfortunately it was only once they'd unrolled their tent and set it out on the ground that Brad and Leanne realised they also needed to clear an area to prevent foliage rubbing on the tent's outer fabric. Removing further vegetation added another foot to the pile, and another hour and a half passed before erection of the tent could commence. Fortunately putting the tent up proved problem free, so by the late afternoon all that remained to do was get the sleeping bags and other essential bits and pieces such as the torch and insect repellent out of the car.

'What are we going to do with that pile of stuff?' Leanne asked as she pointed to the heap of vegetation that had been cleared to make way for the tent, to which Brad replied that they should just chuck it over the surrounding area, and it would disappear amongst the weeds in no time at all.

'I just wondered if we aren't supposed to take it to the green waste area down by the rear gate?'

Brad replied that Leanne might well be correct, but given that the green waste area was about as far from the tent as it was possible to get, that there didn't appear to be a suitably large receptacle or vehicle available with which to transport said waste, and that he was basically knackered - the vegetation was going to turn into compost locally and not in some central waste area just to satisfy Geoffrey's wishes to keep everything neat and tidy.

Brad having made the point fairly forcibly, he and Leanne spent the next fifteen minutes chucking the grass, weeds and bracken they'd removed from their tent's site over the surrounding vegetation, trying to ensure they distributed it as evenly as possible so that it would soon compost down to nothing. That final task complete, Brad and Leanne wandered off to the shower block to get cleaned up and make a start preparing their evening meal.

\*\*\*

The evening was spent in convivial company in the Hidden Lake's clubhouse. George and Gwen had decided to stay in the log cabin and watch Gwen's portable television, so Brad and Leanne finished their dinner and went into the clubhouse for a couple of drinks and a chat with anyone else who happened to be about. As it turned out it was a very quiet evening, and by ten o'clock the last two club members who could be regarded as 'good company' had decided to call it a day and retired to their own cabin. Faced with the prospect of hearing all about two members' recent and absolutely *amazing* holiday in the Algarve, Leanne also decided to call it a day, finished her glass of wine and put down the magazine she'd been skimming through during the evening. Most of the magazine seemed to be concerned with home makeovers, baking and letters from fictitious readers who wanted the magazine's Aunt Sally to solve their sexual problems. Leanne dismissed most of those letters on the basis that, as far as she was concerned, none constituted a real problem. Miss X's partner simply appeared to be slightly over-sexed, Mrs Y's husband just needed a quick squirt with some of that spray you can get from the pharmacy, it was about time Mrs H realised that men actually *enjoy* doing that, and frankly Miss A should stop being so prudish and a life. However the problem that accounted for the most column inches – ironically nothing to do with Mr G's problem – was dedicated to some rather bizarre fetishes, none of which Leanne had ever heard of. In fact a number of the subjects to which those fetishes related were so weird Leanne wasn't entirely convinced they were even genuine. Did some men actually get aroused by cuddly toys? Surely not, although if it were true it might go some way towards explaining the state of Brad's old teddy bear, and why Gwen eventually convinced him to throw the wretched thing out. Mercifully the tatty old bear had been despatched to the dustbin long before Brad's bits started to malfunction, otherwise Leanne would have been seriously concerned.

Fascinated by the article in the woman's magazine - and partly on account of having consumed the best part of half a bottle of red wine in the last hour - Leanne decided that the pair of them should also retire to their overnight accommodation to see if she could coax some life into the annoyingly inert part of her husband's anatomy. Although the cool night air rapidly sobered her up as she and Brad walked back to their tent, Leanne had already decided that it was worthwhile trying a little canoodling under canvas to see if it might have some beneficial effect. So just as soon as the pair of slightly happy campers were back inside their tent - with the tent's zip firmly closed behind them and a battery-powered lantern turned on - Leanne grabbed hold of the tie-cord on her husband's shorts and started undoing it.

'Sweetheart,' Leanne said as she slipped her hand inside Brad's underwear and started fumbling around. 'Do you think you might have some strange fetish or other that you aren't aware of? I'm wondering because that magazine I was reading just now had a whole list of really bizarre fetishes that most people don't even know exist. And if you'd got one and didn't know it – Well I'm sure it could cause all sorts of problems. One day you might be fine, and the next thing you know you could be struck down –permanently down in your case – with some bizarre affliction and be none the wiser. It' not as if there isn't some family history of bizarre sexual behaviour either – I mean, take your father, for example. You aren't going to find many more people with urges quite like his, are you?'

Brad shook his head which didn't help Leanne a great deal because she was fully occupied at the other end.

'Anyway,' continued Leanne, and she wrenched Brad's shorts and underpants down to his ankles without waiting for her husband to reply. 'Once I'd read about these fetishes I started to wonder if maybe that's part of your trouble, and perhaps Dr Raja was right. I mean he is a Doctor after all, and they are supposed to know about these things. Alright, so I know he diagnosed Mr Hamilton's appendicitis as a case of trapped wind, and Mrs Roper's broken hip as 'wear and tear' but anybody can make a mistake.'

'I'm sure I haven't got any odd fetishes,' replied Brad. 'What sort of thing were you thinking of? Lingerie? Leather? Domination? Rubber even?'

'Oh no Brad, nothing simple like that. I'm talking *seriously* weird. For example, I read that some people get turned on by trees. *Dendrophiles*, that's them. You're not one of those though that's for sure, because if you were I'd have noticed something stirring down below when you went off on a wobbly about those willows being cut down. Nor are you a *xylophile* for that matter, because otherwise you'd be off sniffing newly cut timber, and we'd never have got the cabin built. And believe it or not there's another bunch that get a stiffy thinking about stuffed toys of all things! I'm pretty sure you're not one of them. You're not are you? I hate to ask darling, but playing with old Woody Brown Bear never gave you woody anything else I hope, did it? Because if it did sweetheart, we need to talk about it. And soon.'

'Absolutely no way,' replied Brad. 'I'm not any of those, and that last one's just plain weird. But anyway you heard what Doctor Raja said when we visited him. I just need to try and relax more.'

Leanne muttered something about needing to try and get Brad's bit and pieces anything but relaxed pretty damn soon, or she'd have to trawl the Internet for a suitable alternative particularly if he wasn't going to let her play around with that new oscillating multi-tool from B&Q. But just as Leanne finished pondering the few fetishes she'd remembered from the magazine's article another thought crossed her mind. Perhaps Brad was suffering from some work-related fetish but didn't realise it? Was there a name for that Leanne wondered? Maybe it was *workophilia*, but it didn't really make any difference what it was called if he'd got it. And had he got it? Brad had seemed to be in his element when he and that Zoe tart had been engaged in obscure academic arguments about some bloody Caravan Act or other. Had that got Brad's bits moving? There was only one way to find out, so Leanne put her right hand on her husband's chest and started running her index finger around his right nipple.

'Let me run my fingers slowly through your crisp copy of *The Town and Country Planning Act 1990*' darling,' she said, attempting to nibble Brad's right ear lobe at the same time.

'What?'

Leanne moved her hand slowly down Brad's chest, and continued in a southwards direction until she found what she was looking for. Unsurprisingly, it was in its normal condition and as such would not have precluded Brad wearing even his tightest underpants without discomfort, even if they had been boiled in the washing machine until they were only half their normal size.

'I'm permitting your development sweetheart,' she whispered as she tried again to nibble Brad's right ear lobe. 'I'm permitting a large development of this thing here..'

Leanne gripped Brad firmly with her right hand and proceeded to try and develop him in a manner most town planners might find somewhat unorthodox, but to which they would almost certainly not wish to object.

'Does that do it for you darling?' Leanne cooed, as she swapped hands to make herself more comfortable. 'How about we read a copy of *The Town and Country Planning* – open brackets - *Use Classes* – close brackets - *Order 1987* together? Does that get things moving in the right direction?'

'Don't be daft,' replied Brad, although that did nothing to deter Leanne.

'Maybe you like it when I say really dirty things like *The Town and Country Planning* – open brackets - *Development Management Procedure* – close brackets and open a second set of brackets – *England* – close the second set of brackets - *Order 2015*? Do you? Do you, huh? I bet you do sweetheart. I'm going to manage your development Bradley, my darling. I'm going to manage this development until it becomes a *massive* extension to your principal elevation.'

'For goodness sake pack it in woman,' complained Brad who was rapidly becoming fed up with Leanne's ludicrous overtures. 'Where did you pick all that stuff up anyway?'

'From you of course, where do you think? Mostly when you get home at night as a matter of fact. You go off on a rant about something or other not meeting the requirements of the *Community Infrastructure Levy Regulations 2010* or some other such nonsense. I take it all in you know, even about the 'Principal Elevation'.'

'Which is?'

'Normally, but not necessarily, the front elevation of a building. Typically where the front door is located.'

Leanne changed hands again because her arm was getting tired, and she was starting to get cramp.

'And right now I'm giving you permission for the erection of a large temporary extension to your principal elevation - and for a temporary change of use as well now I come to think of it. In fact I'm demanding you erect a large extension pretty bloody soon because my arm is beginning to ache.'

'Look, this is ridiculous.'

'Or maybe you can get it going thinking about really old things? Perhaps that's it. Maybe you're a *gerontophile*? Right, let's give that a try shall we? Here goes: Do you want to thumb through a soiled old copy of the *Planning* – open brackets -*Listed Buildings and Conservation Areas* - close brackets - *Act 1990*. How about that Bradley? Does that get you all red hot and horny for me?'

'Look Leanne, you spouting off all that stuff does nothing for me whatsoever, so just pack it in will you and go to sleep.'

Despite Leanne's efforts, muttering of sweet nothings and a very wet ear lobe it was clear that Brad's errant member remained the physical equivalent of a green-field site, that is to say completely undeveloped.

'I bet it'd get you going if *she* said that stuff to you, wouldn't it? I bet if *she* whispered 'Lets read Article 7 of "*The Town and Country Planning* - open brackets - *General Permitted Development* - close brackets and open a second set of brackets – *England* – close the second set of fucking brackets - *Order 2015*' to you you'd be up and hoisted like a sodding flag up a pole in no time at all.

Brad told Leanne in no uncertain terms that her reciting planning legislation, even by chapter and verse, would have no effect whatsoever on his principle elevation, but by then Leanne was convinced that Zoe might well succeed where she was currently failing.

'I bet that when the pair of you were working together *she* only had to whisper '*Control of Advertisement Regulations 1987*' and you'd be ready to take her wherever she'd let you, even if - as in my case -it was only a one-way trip to bloody Stowmarket. That's it, isn't it? She'd phone you from the other side of the other side of the planning office and say something like "Hey, you horny little stud muffin - never mind my knickers draw, how do you fancy a quick rummage through the *Planning and Compulsory Purchase Act 2004?*" Is that it?'

'Don't be so bloody ridiculous,' snapped Brad, as he briefly recalled his embarrassing experience of phone sex with Miss 'Giselle', three elderly women and the Spaniel.

'So do you find her attractive?'

'I don't know what you mean.'

'It's a very simple question Brad. Do you find that Zoe woman you used to work with attractive? Yes or no.'

It may have been a very simple question, but for some reason or other Brad didn't quite seem to understand what his wife was getting at.

'Attractive in what sort of way?'

'Oh, for heaven's sake Bradley. I'm talking attractive in the 'Bend me over the kitchen table and take me firmly from behind, big boy', sort of way. I'm talking *that* sort of attractive. Now do you get it?'

Brad didn't say anything immediately which told Leanne everything she wanted to know in an instant.

'You do, don't you? You do find her attractive.'

'No, I - Look Leanne, she's not an unattractive woman, but she doesn't – er, 'inflame me' shall we say any more than you..'

'Well thanks a bunch for that,' replied Leanne, who immediately rolled over so that she had her back firmly and resolutely towards her husband.

'I was going to say *any more than you or anyone else can at present,*' explained Brad '*bearing in mind my condition.*'

Leanne sighed and realised that perhaps she'd been rather too quick in jumping to a conclusion.

'Perhaps we'll take you back to Doctor Raja,' she said. 'Or perhaps we'll try and find you another doctor. Goodnight darling.'

With an unspoken apology Leanne turned over and kissed her husband on the cheek. 'Sleep well.'

# Chapter 29

It must have been around two o'clock in the morning when Leanne awoke. She couldn't be entirely sure what time it was because the tent didn't have a clock next to the sleeping bag, it was pitch dark outside, and she couldn't find her torch so that she could have a look at her watch. Brad appeared to be sound asleep although he wasn't snoring, so that wasn't what had woken her up. Leanne could hear the occasional hooting of an owl in the distance, together with the continuous low rumbling of traffic on the A14 in the far distance, neither of which Leanne thought was really loud enough to have awoken her. Perhaps it was just one of those things, or perhaps her mind was trying to tell her something. Whatever had roused her from her sleep Leanne was now wide awake, and there was probably about three hours to go before it started to get light. Whatever else it was trying to tell her, Leanne's mind was certainly letting her know that Brad's condition wasn't going to be sorted out in the near future, so other than going back to sleep the most pleasant way to spend that time - or part of it at least - might just be to indulge in a little very private 'me' time. With part of the spare time before daybreak now accounted for Leanne carefully manoeuvred herself in the sleeping bag so that she could get things underway. She wished she hadn't insisted that she and Brad should zip their two sleeping bags together to make a double. Alright, so it was a practical solution to a rather chilly night, but it was also slightly inconvenient when either of the occupants needed to get up for a pee during the night without disturbing the other, or felt like having a crafty.. – Well let's just say it could be inconvenient.

Faced with the minor inconvenience of being in a double sleeping bag but not wanting to disturb her husband Leanne considered a number of various possibilities. Her favoured option of fiddling around resting face downwards in a soft pillow with her bum sticking up in the air wasn't feasible unless she got out of the sleeping bag, and it was far too bloody cold for that thank you very much. Most other positions involving bodily contortions would probably also necessitate unzipping the sleeping bag or getting out of it altogether, neither of which would provide the warm and cosy environment Leanne was determined to maintain bearing in mind how bloody cold it was outside. So, with most of the more gratifying positions discounted as too cold, too uncomfortable, or too likely to wake Brad up, Leanne pontificated between curling up on her side or laying flat on her back, eventually choosing the latter on the basis that at least she could get her knees apart that way without letting too much chilly night air into the sleeping bag.

Once she'd got herself comfortable Leanne took a couple of deep breaths, and started to try and see if she could recall a couple of her most pleasurable encounters with Brad to help get things underway. Unfortunately nothing immediately sprang to mind, which after a good many years of marriage came as something of a disappointment, so Leanne widened her mental search criteria to include other noteworthy liaisons. It wasn't long before she was fondly recalling that office party – or at least the bits of it during which she was actually conscious - and was soon reliving the moment Monsieur Pierre managed to fondle her buttocks with one hand, while simultaneously undoing her bra strap and rummaging around inside her right-hand 34C cup with the other. In the darkness of the tent Leanne smiled to herself. She recalled thinking at the time 'That was a bloody neat trick Pierre, and for sheer dexterity alone deserves not to go unrewarded.' But even now, all these years later, the only answer Leanne could come up with was that Monsieur Pierre had either got three hands, that he was a magician, or that he.. *Oh bloody hell.* Leanne's daydream suddenly turned into a nightmare as she remembered something her cerebral cortex had long since chosen to tuck away into its deepest vaults. Pierre was at the party with an acquaintance from Leanne's office called Trevor, an accountant who she and most of her girlfriends avoided like the plague if they could on the basis that he was, well, weird. Well weird in fact. The likelihood that Pierre was not the accomplished lover she'd always thought he was, coupled with the distinct possibility that she'd let the weirdo Trevor tinker around with her right nipple shook Leanne out of her state of mild arousal and back into the real world. It didn't matter that she'd disturbed Brad in the process by accidentally kicking him in the back, because any ideas Leanne had about getting the earth under the sleeping bag to move were well and truly scuppered.

'What's wrong?' Brad muttered as Leanne straightened her leg.

'Nothing I, er - I just kicked you by accident. Sorry.'

The majority of Leanne's heightened senses had already returned to their normal levels, but it appeared the olfactory one hadn't. She hadn't noticed it before, but there was no disputing that the air in the tent was nothing short of utterly rank. There was nothing tucked away in the corners of the tent to have gone off - no meat, no fish, and no poultry - and no living things other than Brad and Leanne were confined within its zip-sealed fabric walls. The stench, and it certainly qualified as such, was vaguely reminiscent of Brad and Leanne's bathroom the morning after Brad had unwisely decided that two pints of Guinness on top of a vegetable *bhuna* wouldn't play havoc with his digestion. There was only one explanation, and as far as Leanne was concerned only one culprit.

'You dirty bugger. Fancy doing that when we're in a bloody sleeping bag together.'

'Doing what?'

'Don't pretend it wasn't you.'

'What wasn't?'

'That smell of course. It was you, wasn't it? It's like that time you let one rip when we were in the sauna at Barnsted House. No wonder we've never been back. I shouldn't think they'd let us in again. I'd never been so embarrassed in my life.'

Such evidence as there was against him being purely circumstantial, Brad continued to deny any wrong-doing, suggesting instead that Leanne were to blame but was seeking to frame him for the noxious emission. With both parties continuing to blame the other, and with no other possible candidate, the case of the vile stench appeared destined to remain unresolved. The odour remained undiminished in its intensity irrespective of whoever was to blame, prompting Leanne to turn over in the sleeping bag to see if the air on the side of the tent furthest from Brad was any less pungent. Her first thought was that the inflatable mattress appeared to have sprung a leak, because her shoulder didn't seem to be resting on an air-filled pocket as she would have expected. What was perhaps more disconcerting was that turning over on an air-filled mattress wouldn't normally be expected to result in an audible 'squelch', irrationally suggesting to Leanne that Brad had erected the tent on quicksand.

'Brad!'

'No, I haven't.'

'No, not that. Something's wrong. I think the tent's sinking.'

'Don't be daft Leanne. Go back to sleep for heaven's sake.'

'Get up and see what's going on.'

'Nothing's going on. If you want to get up and have a look outside then be my guest. Here's the torch.'

Brad handed Leanne the torch she'd been unable to locate a few minutes earlier, but try as she might Leanne couldn't find her flip-flops.

'You probably left them outside,' sighed Brad as Leanne crawled around in the tent waving the torch in all four corners in an attempt to find her footwear, and nearly blinding Brad in the process. 'Go out and get them. A bit of damp grass won't hurt you.'

Eventually Leanne pulled down the nylon zip that kept the tent free of mosquitos, and carefully waved the torch around outside to see if she could locate her flip-flops. The first thing she noticed, apart from the fact that the air outside was actually a damn sight colder than it was in the tent, was that Brad's flatulence was every bit as objectionable outside the tent as it was within. The second thing Leanne noticed was that her flip-flops were about three metres away from the tent, which was definitely not where she'd left them. With just the torch to guide her Leanne stepped out of the tent, and onto what she'd thought was grass in order to go and retrieve her footwear. It was only then that she noticed the grass was not only wet, but that it was covered with at least an inch of malodourous slime. If stepping stark naked into a river of putrid slime in the middle of the night when she should have been convulsed with ecstasy wasn't bad enough, Leanne immediately discovered the slime was slippery in the extreme. To make matters worse an unfortunate combination of the slime, a submerged thorn and a temporary loss of balance all conspired to send Leanne crashing to the ground – or more specifically to the slime – where she ended up flat on her back, with the torch casting a shadow of her naked torso on the side of the tent. Knowing what she now did, it was probably just as well that Leanne didn't hear what Brad had to say from within the comfort of the warm sleeping bag.

'Very funny Leanne, but if they're supposed to be mountains then you either need a boob job, to put a bra on, or to keep your arms a bit closer to your sides. How about trying a bunny rabbit instead?'

# Chapter 30

Whoever it was who locked the shower block the previous evening would probably do well to stay silent on the matter. It was bad enough to have fallen over in a river of partly decomposed sewage overspill that had been flowing from the septic tank all night, but then not to have been able to properly wash it off until the following morning was really too much to bear. Brad tried to comfort Leanne when he realised what had happened, but the best he could do was go and get a couple of buckets of water out of the swimming pool and try and wash her down by the light of their torch, although when that proved nigh on impossible he resorted to simply throwing the buckets of water over her. Unfortunately two buckets full proved insufficient to wash off all the slime, so by the time Leanne had dried herself the four towels that were normally sufficient for a weekend at the Hidden Lake Club were well and truly contaminated, as were her flip-flops, the underside of the tent, and the front passenger seat of the car as a result of Leanne's understandable urge to get home as soon as possible. Despite Leanne's insistence that the pair of them depart from the Hidden Lake Club for home and a hot shower immediately, Brad decided that driving naked wasn't a particularly good idea at any time of day or night, so with two plastic bags on his feet he carefully went back inside the tent and retrieved his clothes. In hindsight he should perhaps have retrieved some of Leanne's as well, particularly as a local police patrol with bugger all else to do were curious to know why Brad had a naked woman in his car at four o'clock in the morning, and more to the point why the naked woman was his wife.

***

The following day Brad returned to the Hidden Lake Club to retrieve Leanne's unsoiled clothing and all their other belongings from the tent. With two new plastic bags covering his shoes he waded across the river of slime that was still slowly oozing from the septic tank, and slipped into the tent, leaving his shoes in their bags at the entrance. Once the tent had been emptied Brad undid the guide ropes and tent pegs, and dragged the tent across the grass until it was clear of the vile smelling grey slime. Once on clean grass Brad had planned to get a hose from the club's tool store and wash down the underside of the tent, ready to take it home. He'd also hoped to finish the task without attracting too much attention, but was still trying to fathom out how to connect the hose to an outside tap when Derek turned up.

'Leanne not about?' asked Derek as he stood and watched Brad attempting to screw a hose onto a push-fit connector.

'No, she's at home recovering from last night.'

'Oh, I see. So you've got your little problem sorted out at last then?'

Derek nudged Brad in the side and winked at him with his right eye.

'Good on you mate. Just you get stuck in there my old son.'

'It's not that,' replied Brad, before fully realising what Derek had meant. 'She's.. How do you know about that anyway? It's none of your business. Look Derek, if you really want to know we had a bad night when the bloody septic tank overflowed.'

'Ah, yes, I heard about that,' replied the club's Treasurer, looking at the river of slime which was showing signs of starting to dry in places. 'I was hoping she'd be around because the tank needs looking at again, and with all the experience she got last winter I reckon she's just the girl for the job. After all, with those slender arms of hers she can reach up that overflow pipe as far as anyone. And what's more, the next time the tank needs emptying out and cleaning she'd be able to get inside it no trouble at all. Years ago we used to get Julie and Phil's young lad to do that, but you can't even send kids up a bloody chimney these days, let alone down a septic tank. Health and safety gone bloody mad if you ask me. We used to give him a big bottle of fizzy pop and a box of liquorice allsorts, so it's not as if we weren't making it worth his while.'

Brad promptly told Derek in no uncertain terms that even a bottle of decent champagne and a jumbo box of After Eight wouldn't convince Leanne to shove her arm up the septic tank, let alone get inside it, so he'd just have to find some other sucker.

'I suppose we'd just have to find someone else in that case,' replied Derek. 'But I'm damned if I know who'd do it. It was a bit unfortunate the pair of you were camping there when it overflowed really, because it hasn't done it that badly for years.'

Derek pointed to the area where Brad and Leanne had thrown the vegetation they'd cleared off their camping pitch.

'The problem seems to have been caused by a blockage in one of the pipes to the tank. There's a whole load of grass and weeds been chucked over there, and some of it's probably got stuck somewhere. Still, on the plus side at least you know why they used to call that part of the site 'Shite Alley'.'

'You bloody well told me we'd be upwind of the septic tank,' Brad complained as he recalled Derek's sales pitch, although he said nothing about the origins of the material Derek had suggested might have caused the blockage.

'You were upwind of it Brad, unfortunately you were also downhill of it. And therein lays the problem -gravity. The other problem we've got – I've got – is who I'm going to get to sort that tank out. It's almost easier to find someone to serve on the Committee than it is to get them anywhere near that damn tank.'

'Maybe you could incentivise them by offering a guarantee they wouldn't get co-opted to serve on the Committee for the next five years?' suggested Brad, which Derek thought might be a sensible idea.

Brad decided not to engage Derek in conversation any longer, because it appeared inevitable that to do so would involve hitting him sooner or later. Instead, he just told Derek that he'd things to do, and needed to get on doing them. One thing was for sure, he and Leanne wouldn't be pitching their tent downstream of the septic tank's overflow pipe again, even if it was upwind of the tank itself. Unfortunately that begged the question of where they were going to erect the tent if, that was, Leanne was prepared to ever set foot in it again.

Once he'd sorted out how to fit the hose onto the tap it didn't take Brad long to clear the slime off the underside of the tent. The sewn-in groundsheet turned out to be a blessing, because it meant that only the waterproof underside had been soiled, and with the hose turned on full blast the offending material was soon washed off. With the tent lying upside down on the ground and slowly drying out there wasn't a great deal more Brad could do, so he decided to go and see how Gwen and George were getting on in the log cabin.

The difference in his parents' enjoyment of the previous night to that of his wife couldn't have been more different. Gwen and George had made themselves completely at home in Brad and Leanne's log cabin, and were in the process of customising it as he arrived.

'Oh hello darling,' exclaimed Gwen as she saw Brad arrive. 'Kissee kissee.'

'Hello Mother. Kissee kissee to you too.'

'Come in dear, come in, I've got something very exciting to show you.'

Gwen beckoned frantically to her son, then took his left hand and virtually dragged him into the cabin before realising that he was alone.

'Is Leanne still in the tent? Oh, run back and get her dear and I'll show you both together.'

'No Mother, she's at home. We had a really bad experience last night so I took her home and I've just come back again this morning.'

'Oh that's a shame dear. Nothing of a sexual nature I hope? Because if it is I'm sure I can help sort it out for you. I've had plenty of experience with your father after all. What is it dear? You can tell me about it.'

'No, I..'

Brad didn't get a chance to explain the events of the previous evening before George attempted to provide an explanation of an entirely different nature.

'Problems of a sexual nature? Him? Our son Bradley? Don't be daft woman. He hasn't been able to get it ..'

Brad didn't wait for his father to spell out the precise nature of his little problem, and although he tempered his description of the grey slime's ingredients he might have done well to have considered his words rather more carefully.

'She got covered in gallons of pee if you must know.'

'Oh dear,' replied Gwen, shaking her head from side to side. 'You really are going to need to find a head doctor for that I'm afraid.'

'You don't understand Mother.'

'No dear, I don't. In fact I never have. Fortunately your father's never shown any inclination towards that sort of activity I'm very pleased to say. He's shown more than a passing interest in just about every other variant you can *imagine* – and indeed some you probably can't – but that, never. You can't begin to imagine how worried I was when we were at that hotel in Jamaica. I mean to say, it was a lovely hotel, but when I heard they were offering free non-motorised water sports I really thought I was going to have all sorts of trouble with him.'

Brad sighed as he realised just how difficult it was going to be to explain the previous night's events to his parents without it sounding like he and Leanne were working their way through an advanced sex manual.

'As I was saying, the septic tank overflowed and ran underneath our tent, and then Leanne slipped over and got covered in slime when she stepped outside to see what was going on. Then we discovered the shower block was locked so she couldn't get herself clean, and that's when we went home and got her all cleaned up. That's all.'

'Sounds like more than enough to me,' said George. 'Talking of emulsion, do you like the décor?'

'Décor?'

George pointed to each of the walls of the log cabin in turn.

'That was going to be *my* surprise,' said Gwen, and she slapped George on the arm.

Brad looked around the room. Each of the four walls had been painted a different colour, apart from one wall which had been covered in floral wallpaper that looked as if it had last graced a wall in the early 1970s.

'Isn't it lovely dear?' said Gwen, beaming from ear to ear.

'It's very, well, to be honest Mother it looks like an old folks' home.'

'Well thank you dear,' replied Gwen. 'That's exactly what we wanted.'

'No Mother, I meant it's a bit.. Oh, never mind. I just wished you'd asked us first that's all. It's not really to my taste and it's not going to be to Leanne's either, so once you've..'

Brad managed to stop himself from saying anything more about future events, and changed the subject to something more palatable.

'So once you've finished doing what you're doing to the walls perhaps you'd leave it at that?'

'You don't want me to finish fixing the roof then?' said George.

'What do you mean 'Fixing the roof'? What's wrong with the roof?'

George pointed to a timber that ran from left to right along the length of the cabin viewed from where Brad was standing.

'That purlin's broken,' he said. 'You can see it from here. Look, split right across it is. That needs repairing or part of the roof could collapse. That other one there isn't much better either. The timbers are far too thin to take the weight. That's the problem.'

Brad didn't think to ask his father why the roof timbers had suddenly become inadequate, particularly since they'd been perfectly fit for purpose when they'd been fitted as part of Dunwich Hoo's inventory. If he had asked, he might have started to wonder exactly what his parents were doing to the cabin to warrant structural reinforcement of the roof timbers.

'Oh, I see,' he said. 'Well if it needs doing then, yes, please finish that as well. But just leave it that please. No other modifications if you don't mind. Okay?'

George nodded, and said he wouldn't start any other works - structural or otherwise -without first discussing them with what decided to call his 'landlords'.

# Chapter 31

Neither Brad nor Leanne knew exactly what time it was when the phone in the lounge rang, because despite Brad having bought the correct sized battery the silly sod – to use Leanne's terminology – hadn't yet fitted it. It was certainly something before four o'clock in the morning because it was still dark outside and the dawn chorus hadn't yet started. Brad was tempted to let the phone ring until the caller hung up, but on the basis that the caller might be one or other of his parents he decided he couldn't risk it, so he got out of bed without waking Leanne and made his way to the lounge.

'Have I reached the household of Leanne Marie Dixon?' asked the caller. 'Wife of Mr Bradley Dixon, the only son of Mr George Dixon and Mrs Gwen Dixon.'

Brad sighed, realising the call was almost certainly not of any great importance.

'What is it Mother?'

'Oh hello dear, kissee kissee. You don't sound like Leanne to me.'

'That's because I'm not.'

'Well that's no good dear. I need to speak to Mrs Leanne Dixon, wife of Mr Bradley Dixon.'

'That would indeed be the Bradley Dixon to whom you *are* speaking. Now what is it you want Mother?'

'I want to speak to Leanne dear. Now go and find her for me, chop chop.'

'She's asleep,' replied Brad.

'Well wake her up then dear. Wake her up. Just put a cool hand somewhere she wouldn't normally expect it and she'll be wide awake in no time. Believe me dear, I've had many years of experience so I know about these things.'

'I'm not waking her up at this time of night, whatever time it actually is.'

'It's important dear. I need to tell her something, now go and wake her up. There's a good boy.'

Brad sighed again. There was no point arguing with Gwen because he knew she'd never give up, and would contentedly be arguing away until daybreak. So reluctantly Brad made his way back to the bedroom, and slipped one hand under the duvet and moved it around until he found warm flesh. Whether or not Leanne had previously been sound asleep she wasn't now, although it was clear to Brad she wasn't fully aware of what he was doing.

'Mm, you haven't done that for a while darling. Mm, that's lovely. Mm, you..'

There was a brief silence as Leanne's level of consciousness increased to the point that she realised all was not what it seemed. Still resting on her side Leanne turned her head so that she was facing the ceiling.

'That's your finger, isn't it?'

'Mother want's to speak to you.'

'We'll start this conversation again, shall we? Bradley, have you got a finger between my bum cheeks? And if so, why? And if it isn't your finger - then thank you for the effort dear, but it's even smaller than it used to be, so perhaps we'll take a rain check. Now, can I get back to sleep or was there a reason for this unexpected intrusion into one of my more personal spaces?'

'I've got Mother on the phone and she wants to speak to you.'

'To me?'

'To you.'

'Gwen wants to speak to me?'

'You got it at last.'

'What about?'

'I've no idea, but she said it was important.'

Brad was slightly surprised that Leanne didn't object to the idea of getting out of her bed and simply said 'Oh' before pulling back the duvet and putting her slippers on.

'You might be some time,' said Brad. 'So I'd put a dressing gown on if I were you.'

Leanne muttered something about that being a good idea, and slipped a T shirt over her head before making her way into the lounge to find out what was so important it couldn't wait until the morning.

'Hello,' she said, picking up the phone's handset.

'Is that Mrs Leanne Marie Dixon? Wife of Mr Bradley Dixon and dearly beloved daughter-in-law of Gwen and George Dixon.'

'Er, yes, it is,' replied Leanne, slightly unsure of how to respond to a phone call from her mother –in-law at that time of night.

'Jolly good. Now then dear, I just need to ask you a security question to make quite sure I'm speaking to the correct person. This call may be recorded for security and training purposes. Now then dear, on what date were you and my darling son Mr Bradley Dixon married?'

'May 18th 1990,' replied Leanne, without even having to think.

'I'm sorry dear, I'm afraid that's not the correct answer.'

'Of course it is Gwen. I know when my wedding anniversary is dear, believe me.'

'Well, does the date October 22nd, 1805 mean anything to you?'

Leanne told Gwen that nothing immediately sprang to mind apart from it being the day after the Battle of Trafalgar, which immediately caused her to remember something Brad had said in a previous conversation with his mother.

'I'm just going to put the handset down for a second Gwen,' she said. 'Don't go away, I'll be right back.'

Leanne tiptoed downstairs and into the kitchen, where she opened the freezer door. In the top drawer she found an ice pack which she took out and carefully put on the kitchen worktop. Then she shut the freezer door and tiptoed back upstairs again but, instead of continuing her conversation with Gwen, Leanne took the ice pack into her bedroom where she found Brad fast asleep and lying flat on his back. Revenge was going to be sweet indeed. Leanne slipped the ice pack under the duvet until she was holding it approximately a foot above her husband's groin. Then she let go.

'That!' Leanne shouted as Brad almost leapt out of the bed. 'That is for forgetting our wedding anniversary, you useless little shit. And talking of which - I'm going shopping in the morning, and I'm buying myself a big bottle of something expensive and gorgeously smelly, to cover the lingering effects of something horrible and disgustingly malodourous. And you, yes you, are going to pay for it. And if you ever forget the significance of May 18th again I promise I will do everything I can to put you at the bottom of that fucking septic tank wearing nothing but a pair of cement boots. Capiche?

Leanne took it as read that her husband fully understood the potential consequences of forgetting their wedding anniversary again, and returned to her unfinished conversation with her mother-in-law.

'I'm sorry about that Gwen. I just needed a quick word with my dear husband about something. Now, what was it you wanted to tell me?'

'I needed to let you know how important my family is, and how much you all mean to me. You, your husband Bradley – that's my son by the way – my daughter Zena..'

'Zara,' said Leanne. 'Your daughter's name is Zara.'

'Is it? Oh well Zara then. And of course her dear children – my grandchildren – Jimmy and Edwina.'

'Jeffrey and Tina.'

'Who are?'

'Your grand-children. Their names are Jeffrey and Tina.'

'Well fancy you knowing that,' replied Gwen. 'You are clever. Anyway the point is you all need to know how much you mean to George and me. I'm sure you've heard stories about people not telling their loved ones how much they care about them, and before they know it they've been run over by a bus and then it's too late. I am of course talking *metaphorical* buses, because I know how infrequent rural services are these days. So the chances of actually being run over by a real rural bus are actually fairly slim. I suppose it's far more likely that you'd be hit by a car, or a juggernaut with Polish or Bulgarian licence plates, a horse box, a tractor or even a motorcycle and sidecar- but that's not what people say is it? No, they say they've been run over by a bus. Of course they don't actually say *they've* been run over by a bus, because they wouldn't be here to tell the story would they? But you're clever enough to understand what I mean. I'd probably have to explain it to young Bradley, but you're clever enough to work it out all by yourself. The *real* point is that it would be so sad if anything were to happen to you, and you didn't know how important you are to us. So while it was fresh in my mind I thought I'd phone around the family to let you all know.'

'That's very sweet of you Gwen,' replied Leanne, who was beginning to realise she was getting cold and wished she'd put on more than just a thin T shirt.

'And you will come for tea tomorrow, won't you? We'll be at home because the forecast isn't wonderful and it's much easier to do food there.'

Leanne said that she and Brad would love to go over and have tea, provided that Gwen let Leanne help her prepare the food, and that under no circumstances was she to go to too much trouble or prepare anything from her 'Premier' range. Leanne's insistence that Gwen should not go to too much trouble was probably as much in her own interests as that of her mother-in-law, because it must have taken her a further fifteen minutes to wear Gwen down to the point where she finally agreed to let Leanne help in the kitchen. By this time Leanne was absolutely perishing cold and beginning to fear that she'd be getting close to hyperthermia if she didn't get off the phone pretty soon. Eventually Gwen conceded defeat and said Leanne could help make the sandwiches, so Leanne wished Gwen goodnight – or at least what was left of it – and went back to bed. It'd serve Brad right if she did stick her cold hands on him to warm them up, or if she pulled off her T shirt and wrapped her arms around him so she could feel the warmth of his body next to hers. One way or another Leanne knew she'd soon be warm and cosy, and she would have been if only Brad hadn't put the thawing ice pack on her side of the bed.

# Chapter 32

The following day Brad and Leanne drove over to George and Gwen's bungalow in the early afternoon ready to take tea with them as promised. As a precaution against Gwen going back on her word and preparing a selection of her 'Premier' sandwiches Brad drove to his parents via a local supermarket where he bought two packs of ready-made bacon, lettuce and tomato, and two over-priced slices of organic carrot cake. Neither Brad nor Leanne had thought about having a back-up plan before they left home, and it was only as they drove past the supermarket that Leanne belatedly suggested it might be a good idea. The suggestion was in fact so belated that Brad ended up taking a minor detour by driving to the next roundabout and doubling back on himself.

'We can stick them in the freezer if we don't need them,' Leanne suggested as she and Brad continued their journey. 'But I think it's probably a good idea to have something with us, just in case. I know your strange father likes pilchard and strawberry jam, but I'm not even going to try it. What was it Gwen made that trifle with?'

'Salad cream.'

'That was it - Salad cream, and raspberries, pickled onions and gherkins. Honestly.'

'Well she promised to let you help in the kitchen this time, so at least you can keep an eye on what's going on as well as what's going in. And she promised not to do anything from her 'Premier' range either, so if you just keep it simple you'll be fine.'

***

Despite their minor detour to the supermarket Brad and Leanne arrived at George and Gwen's bungalow slightly ahead of schedule. There didn't appear to be anybody about, so Brad and Leanne sat in their car for a few minutes rather than disturb a couple of elderly pensioners who might have been taking an afternoon nap, or been busy preparing for their guests' arrival. Eventually Brad decided they'd waited long enough, so he got out of the car and walked up the drive to his parents' front door.

The doorbell had almost finished playing its distorted version of Colonel Bogey when Brad heard Gwen's voice through the letterbox.

'Whatever you're trying to sell we don't want it. You should be ashamed of yourself, trying to con a veteran of the Malaya conflict and his elderly wife into parting with their money. Now go away or I'll set the dog on you.'

Brad remembered what George had told him previously about going around to the back of the house because the rear door was always open, but he didn't want to risk startling his parents or disturbing them if they hadn't been ready.

'Hello Mother. It's only us. I hate to be a pedant but you haven't actually got a dog these days.'

'Oh, hello dear. I didn't realise it was you. Kissee kissee. Just wait there a moment will you please. I just need to get George to unlock the door because I can't reach the top bolt. George! George!'

By now Leanne had joined her husband so the pair of them waited a couple of minutes while Gwen went to try and find George. She soon returned although George remained unavailable.

'He's in the toilet dear, so if you just ..'

'We'll come around the back Gwen,' said Leanne, before Gwen could tell her the door would be unlocked. 'The door's probably open.'

'Fancy you knowing that dear. My word you are a clever young lady.'

\*\*\*

As soon as she'd got indoors and taken her shoes off Leanne gave her mother in law a hug and kissed her on the cheek, and Brad did likewise.

'Hello George,' Leanne said without offering him the same physical contact. Time was that Leanne had been far more inclined towards her father in law, but that was before she and Gwen had patched up their differences. It was also before George had decided a thorough grope of Leanne's buttocks with one hand and a fumble around the inside of her sweater with the other was appropriate in the way of a reciprocal greeting.

'Hello dear. Don't I get a kiss?'

Leanne blew George a kiss and told him that would have to do as she thought she might be starting a bit of a cold, and didn't want to give it to him.

'And George - Before you ask a shag's right out of the question, and if you were tempted to ask then let me tell you the question's right out of order too.'

The assembled foursome all laughed, Leanne because she'd completed the necessary greetings without being molested, and George because Leanne had wittily pre-empted his next question. Gwen had laughed because her clever daughter-in-law had put George firmly in his place even if she had used a phrase Gwen would never herself have uttered, well not in polite company anyway. But that really didn't matter today because the grandchildren – Jeremy and Edwina, or was it Jeffrey and Tina? – weren't about to hear it. Even Brad laughed, although his nervous laughter had more to do with Leanne avoiding the subject of her husband's necessary equipment being 'out of order' rather than anything else.

The greetings completed Gwen and Leanne made their way into the kitchen while Brad and George made themselves comfortable in the lounge. Brad sat himself down on the settee but hadn't read more than the headlines on the local newspaper when George decided to ask him one of his usual questions.

'Did I ever tell you about the time I was out in Malaya?'

'Yes Father, you did.'

'It was while I was in the Navy. Best time of my life that was..'

'Until you met Mother.'

'Until I met your mother. Well, to tell the truth, I.. How did you know?'

'You've told me about it many a time.'

'Oh, I see. Well, did I tell you about the time me and my mates were in Mr Patel's Penang Passion Parlour, and we ended up having a competition with a bunch of Germans to see who could shoot their..'

'Yes, you did, and I really don't want to hear about it again, thank you Father. It really was quite the most disgusting and frankly implausible story you've come up with yet.'

'Oh. Well how about the time I was out there and Mr Patel tried to palm me off – if you'll excuse the phrase – with a Miss Susie instead of my favourite young lady Miss Lucy Lee? Did I tell you about that?'

'Yes, you did.'

'Well how about when me and my mates were out in Japan, and we ended up eating a buffet dinner off this naked woman's back? Did I tell you about that?'

'Yes, you did. It's called Nyotaimori, and as I recall you ended up that evening being thrown out of the premises when your mate accidentally speared the poor woman up the backside with a chopstick.'

'Well bugger me,' said George as he realised he'd have to delve deeper into his repertoire if he was to regale any stories his son hadn't yet had the pleasure of hearing.

\*\*\*

Despite having been told not to go to any trouble Gwen had been busy in the kitchen. She hadn't yet put made the sandwiches, but she'd buttered the bread – Leanne established it was actually butter before proceeding much further with preparation of the meal – and had prepared the sandwich fillings.

'This one's pilchard and strawberry jam,' Gwen proudly announced as she picked up a glass bowl with a sheet of cling-film covering a revoltingly lumpy red gunge. 'It's George's favourite.'

'Well in that case why don't we let George have all of it as a special treat for looking after you,' suggested Leanne. She pointed to a second glass bowl and one made of white plastic. 'What are those two?'

'That one's corned beef and peanut butter, and that one..' Gwen pointed to the white plastic bowl. 'Is tuna and mayonnaise.'

'Tuna and mayonnaise?'

'Yes dear, that's what I said - tuna and mayonnaise.'

Leanne picked up the plastic bowl and pulled the cling-film off the top.

'What's the mayonnaise made of Gwen?' she asked, after sniffing the contents.

'Well, to tell the truth dear I don't really know. Don't tell George will you, but it's not actually home-made. Look.'

Gwen pulled open a door in one of the kitchen units, revealing a waste bin inside. Then she put her hand into the bin and pulled out an empty plastic bottle.

'Egg, oil, vinegar, stabiliser, natural colouring, antioxidant.'

'And you haven't put anything else in it? Not custard powder perhaps? Or mustard?'

'No dear.'

'Bulls' semen?'

'Don't be silly dear.'

'Sorry Gwen, but after that episode with your freezer I just thought I'd make doubly sure. So it's just flaked tuna and mayonnaise mixed together?'

Gwen nodded. 'Tuna, mayonnaise, and salt and pepper. That's all dear.'

Leanne smiled. 'That's smashing Gwen, I love tuna sandwiches.'

***

George was still trying to find a story Brad hadn't previously heard when Leanne carried the first of the plates of sandwiches into the lounge.

'Well, what about the time I tried to cover Miss Lucy Lees' lady bits with whipped cream and glace cherries?'

'You've told me that one too. The cream went rancid.'

'Well bugger me.'

'We're eating off our laps this evening,' Leanne said as she handed out the tea plates, the first of which she gave to George. 'This one's yours George – Pilchard and strawberry jam. Here's yours Brad – Corned beef and peanut butter. You can scrape off the peanut butter if you don't want it.'

'What are you having?' asked Brad, as Leanne sat herself down.

'Tuna mayo. There wasn't enough for two. Sorry.'

Brad would have much preferred tuna mayo to corned beef, with or without peanut butter. He didn't much care for corned beef, and for that matter he didn't much care for peanut butter either, and a combination of the two sounded as if it had come straight out of Hell's kitchen.

'And Gwen's having.. What are you having Gwen?'

'I'm having one of these dear,' replied Gwen, holding up one of the packs of sandwiches Brad had picked up en-route. 'They're supposed to be eaten by today so I don't want them to go to waste. I don't actually remember buying them to be honest.'

Brad looked at Leanne, and Leanne looked at Brad, but neither said anything.

'There's cake and other nibbles in the kitchen, so you can all help yourselves when you're ready' Leanne said as the others all took a bite of their sandwiches, one more gingerly than the others. Leanne took a bite of her own sandwich but then remembered she hadn't finished reciting the day's menu.

'There's also ice cream and..*aargh, oh, urgh, yuk!*'

Brad didn't get a chance to ask Leanne what was wrong with her sandwich, because she rushed past him and into the kitchen, where she turned the cold water tap on full blast and stuck her head under it.

'Well fancy that,' said Gwen. 'Well I never. And she told me she *likes* tuna and mayonnaise.'

It was clear that Leanne was in no fit state to confirm or deny Gwen's statement, because she still had her head under the cold water tap, and all Brad could make out was something like 'Oh, oh, urrgh!' as she repeatedly filled her mouth with water, and then spat it out again. Brad wasn't sure what - if anything - he could do, but he went into the kitchen to try and find out what was going on, and make sure that Leanne wasn't in danger of choking. After a dozen or so more large mouthfuls of water Leanne eventually took her head away from the cold tap and, with bright red blood-shot eyes and make up running down her face, she stared at Brad.

'What's wrong?' Brad asked.

'What in the name of *fuck* was in those sandwiches? It damn near took my head off!'

'Tuna and mayonnaise!' shouted Gwen from the lounge. 'Tuna, mayonnaise, salt and pepper. You said you *liked* tuna and mayonnaise.'

Leanne put her head over the sink so that a long dribble of saliva didn't run down the front of the kitchen units. 'Just how much bloody salt and pepper did you put in Gwen?'

'Two teaspoons full dear. One of each.'

Brad looked around the kitchen and spotted a pile of cutlery ready to be washed up. Then he picked up the only spoon in the pile and took it into the lounge.

'Is this the spoon you used Mother?'

Gwen nodded. 'Yes dear, that's the one.'

'That, Mother, is a tablespoon, and a large one at that. Are you saying that you put a heaped one of these into the tuna?'

'Yes dear. Two actually, one of salt and one of pepper.'

Brad shook his head in disbelief and started to walk back to the kitchen, but before he got there Leanne's stomach reacted in the only way it knew how to a massive overload of salt. If Leanne hadn't been quite so badly affected she might have fancied that spare pack of ready-made BLT instead of the tuna, but with her stomach having just violently expelled her lunch, breakfast and most of last night's dinner into the kitchen sink Brad decided he wouldn't suggest it right now.

# Chapter 33

Following her near salt-poisoning experience Leanne spent the next two days in bed, venturing up at regular intervals to get herself another large glass of water, and then to go for a pee about twenty minutes later. As soon as they'd got home -but only after he'd wiped a pile of yesterday's breakfast and lunch out of the passenger foot well - Brad had looked up the symptoms of salt poisoning on the Internet to find out exactly what he should do if Leanne's condition deteriorated. A raging thirst was nothing to worry about – hell, he only needed a packet of crisps before he fancied a pint or two - but if Leanne started getting confused, or her muscles started twitching, or she started having spasms, or went into a coma, or stopped breathing then he'd probably have to give Dr Raja a call. Fortunately by the third day Leanne had got over the worst of it, and was left with minor symptoms such as lethargy and irritability, convincing Brad that she had totally recovered on the basis that she was acting pretty much as normal.

***

It must have been around three thirty in the morning when the phone in Brad and Leanne's lounge rang. Brad had no idea what time it was because although he'd bought the correct type of batteries and fitted them into the bedside clock, he'd inserted the batteries back to front and had knackered the clock's delicate electronic circuitry. So with no-one to blame for the clock's demise but himself, Brad wearily got out of bed and made his way into the lounge to answer the phone. As with previous calls at this time of the night Brad felt slightly apprehensive. No-one in their right mind would call him unless it was a matter of importance, or unless they were in a time zone many hours ahead or behind GMT. As soon as he answered the phone Brad realised that he need not have been unduly concerned, and that the caller fell into the first of the two categories.

'Have I reached the household of Mr Bradley Dixon and that of his wife Mrs Leanne Marie Dixon?' asked the caller. 'That is to say the household of the only son of Mr George Dixon and Mrs Gwen Dixon, and of their recently debilitated daughter in law.'

'What is it Mother?'

'Kissee kissee dear. Don't worry, it's nothing serious. I was just wondering how my darling daughter-in-law is now?'

'You're phoning at this time of night to ask how Leanne is?' replied Brad, as a precursor to asking Gwen what the hell she thought she was playing at.

'Yes dear, that's the one. Why, how many wives have you got?'

'Just the one Mother, and sometimes that's more than enough.'

'Really Bradley, what a thing to say about your darling wife. How is she anyway?'

'She's a lot better, thank you. But why on earth are you calling at this time of night?'

'When you get to my age you need to take every chance you get dear. I'd just 'seen' to George in a manner of speaking, and for some reason it made me wonder how Leanne was. So I thought I'd better call to find out.'

'I see. Well I'm pleased to say she's back to her old self.'

'Jolly good. So be a good boy and go and get her.'

'She's asleep Mother, and I'm not waking her up just so that the pair of you can a have a bit of a girlie chat. If you want to speak to her I'll ask her to call you in the morning. How's that?'

'Who is it?' shouted a voice from the bedroom, to which Brad immediately replied that it was his mother, an action he would not have taken had his brain been fully co-ordinated with his mouth.

'You just told me she was asleep,' replied Gwen, who was evidently a lot more awake than her son. 'Now I'd like a word with her. So you just be a good little boy and go and get her for me, or I'll have to spank your little botty the next time I see you.'

Brad walked back to the bedroom and explained to Leanne that Gwen wanted a word with her. No, he didn't know what it was about and, no, he hadn't asked her because if he had he'd still be on the phone. But the bottom line was that it would probably be far quicker for Leanne to talk to Gwen than for Brad to argue the toss with her. Grudgingly Leanne got out of bed, pulled a T shirt over her head, and went to find out exactly why Gwen wanted a word with her daughter-in-law at fuck knows what time o'clock in the morning.

'Hello Gwen. What's wrong sweetheart?'

'Hello dear. Nothing's wrong. I'm just calling to see if you could do me a favour. Now, before we start I just need to ask you a couple of security questions.'

'No Gwen dear, you don't. You know full well it's me - now exactly what is that favour you wanted me to do for you? So let's have no more of this security question nonsense, alright? Now, what is it you need me to do?'

There was a brief silence as Gwen pondered whether she should skip her usual bizarre security question preamble and proceed with a normal conversation, or whether she should stick to her guns.

'I, er, I was wondering if you could do me a favour please?'

'Yes, I know. So what is it you want me to do?'

'I, er, I was wondering if perhaps you could pick up a prescription for me from the surgery the next time you come to the club? George and I are up here for another three nights, and I'll have run out of my medicine by then. It just needs collection, so do you think you could do that for me?'

'Of course I can,' replied Leanne, wondering why Gwen had asked her and not Brad.

'I'd have asked Bradley, but he's got a memory like a sieve so I thought it best if I ask you.'

Leanne said she understood, and that of course she'd pick up Gwen' prescription – tomorrow in fact - and if that was all, well, goodnight Gwen and sleep tight.

'So what did she want?' Brad asked as Leanne got back into bed.

'She just wants me to pick up a prescription for her.'

'And she phoned in the middle of the night to ask you that?'

'You're beginning to sound like I used to,' replied Leanne, although she omitted to mention her own inimitable way of responding to unwanted callers during the night-time hours. 'I'm going that way tomorrow anyway so I can pick up the prescription, and then we'll take it with us when we go to the club on Sunday.'

*** 

The following day Leanne did as she'd promised and collected Gwen's prescription from Dr Raja's surgery on the way back from doing the shopping. In fact she forgot all about it until she was nearly home, so as things turned out the errand actually took her well out of her way. But that didn't matter, because Leanne had promised she'd do as Gwen had asked, and she wasn't going to break her promise under any circumstances. Leanne cursed her forgetfulness as she made a rather unwise U turn in a side-street, because the schools would have just turned out and parking at Dr Raja's surgery was a nightmare at the best of times. Realising that trying to park at the surgery would be a pain in the bum – and then some – Leanne decided to park on one of the side streets in the new housing development just around the corner from the surgery, and walk the last couple of hundred yards. It was a wise move, and Leanne felt decidedly smug as she walked past a queue of cars all waiting to get parked at the surgery's pathetically under-sized car park. In fact she'd collected a paper bag containing Gwen's prescription, signed for it as the patient's representative, and convinced the cashier that she didn't have to pay for it as Gwen was well over 60 before a particularly distinctive vehicle she'd seen on the walk to the surgery had even made it into the car park.

All Leanne had to do now was walk back to her car and then drive home with Gwen's prescription, but for some reason or other she didn't. Quite what it was that was so intriguing about a white paper bag with a large green cross on it Leanne had no idea, so maybe it was simply the act of carrying a bag and not knowing precisely what that bag contained that made Leanne decide she had to look inside. In fact the contents of the paper bag were decidedly unexciting, and comprised just a small cardboard box with the name of the drug written in black letters on the side. But it was the name of the drug that caught Leanne's attention - Amoxicillin.

Leanne stopped walking, took the box out of the paper bag, and then read the name of the drug again to make sure she hadn't misread it the first time. It still said 'Amoxicillin' which Leanne was pretty sure wasn't a painkiller. In fact she was almost certain that Dr Raja had prescribed it to her when she'd had some discomfort from a nasty urinary infection a couple of years ago, and which Brad had wrongly attributed to Leanne changing the washing powder she used to launder her underwear to a cheaper brand. Standing in the street was hardly the place to be reading the instruction leaflet from a packet of pills – particularly since they weren't hers - so Leanne walked back to her car. Once inside she opened the box, took out a small leaflet, and started to read all about Gwen's medication.

***

'Why do you think Dr Raja's prescribing Gwen a general purpose antibiotic?' Leanne asked Brad when he arrived home from work that evening.

'I don't know,' replied Brad. 'Perhaps she's got an infection. That would seem a logical enough solution, wouldn't you say? After all that's what it's for.'

'But it's not going to help control pain, is it?'

'Well perhaps it's for something else. Look, if Mother was going to run out of painkillers in the next couple of days she'd have said, wouldn't she?'

Leanne agreed that Gwen would have asked her to pick up any other medication she was getting short of, provided of course that she'd realised it would soon be needed. But perhaps Gwen hadn't realised and would run out in the next couple of days? Or maybe the pharmacy had got the prescription wrong? Or maybe Dr Raja had screwed up – and of the various possibilities that seemed the most likely. Whatever the case, Leanne resolved to find out the next time she saw Gwen.

# Chapter 34

Brad hadn't really anticipated going to the Hidden Lake Club that Saturday, particularly as the weather forecast wasn't particularly good. Quite why they couldn't have waited until the Sunday he wasn't sure, but Leanne had got a bee in her bonnet about checking Gwen's medication as a matter of urgency, and so that was that. As it turned out the weather was a lot better than anticipated, and as a result quite a few of the club's other members had also decided to spend the day there. In fact the first thing Brad noticed as he drove up the driveway to the club's car park was the number of cars parked along the sides. The second thing was that the entrance to the car park was blocked by a large lorry with a load of building materials on the rear, which went some way to explaining why member's cars were parked even more haphazardly than usual.

It didn't take Brad and Leanne long to find out why there was a lorry in the club's car park. Before they'd reached the clubhouse to sign in Brad and Leanne ran into Bill who explained - much to Brad's relief - that the lorry wasn't delivering log cabins, mobile homes, or anything else destined for human habitation. Unfortunately Brad's second worst fears were confirmed when Bill explained the materials on the back of the lorry were destined to be delivered to Derek.

'So what the hell does he want all that timber for?' Brad asked as soon as Bill had divulged the name of the purchaser.

'Apparently he's decided he needs a cart lodge,' explained Bill. 'To park his car in and stop the bloody pigeons from crapping on it. There's been one hell of an argument about it, I can tell you. He's going to put it next to his log cabin, so I've heard.'

'A cart?' asked Leanne. 'Did you say Derek's got a cart? What sort of a cart?'

Brad explained that a 'cart lodge' was a type of building traditional to the area and historically used to keep a horse-drawn cart in, but now seemingly used to describe an open-fronted building intended to house the family car.

'You mean he wants a garage,' suggested Leanne, to which Brad replied that Derek probably did – particularly if it was going to have an up-and-over door on the front - but like many would-be 'cart lodge' owners he was far too pretentious to describe it thus.

'Anyway,' said Bill as he started to conclude his abbreviated history. 'Now that Derek's having a cart lodge there's a whole load of others suddenly decided they need the same. Most of the bloody Committee in fact. There were a whole bunch of complaints from the prospective owners of the second row of cabins – or mobile homes, or whatever they end up with – that these new 'cart lodge' things would block their views of the lake. So those members said they needed to either raise the land so they still had their views, or they'd have to have two-storey cabins. A couple of them even wanted balconies so they could enjoy an evening G&T overlooking the lake, the pretentious old sods.'

'So what does Zoe reckon to all this?' asked Brad.

'Nobody's seen or heard from her since all this kicked off, which is hardly surprisingly really. It's like the bloody Klondike out there, what with all the 'Gold' members staking their claims to a site, all the 'Silver' members applying to become 'Gold' members so they can stake their own claim, and all the 'Bronze' members getting the hump and pissing off to Westlands because they know damn well they'll never be able to get on the 'log cabin ladder'. So it's hardly surprising that Zoe's keeping her head down when you think about it.'

'And her fat wobbling arse,' muttered Leanne, although neither Brad nor Bill heard her.

Brad didn't say anything, but he didn't need to for Leanne to realise what he was thinking. Just as soon as Bill had finished explaining about the cart lodges, and the rush to upgrade membership Leanne found herself reading her husband's body language. Roughly translated it said: *I knew this would happen, and that's why I didn't tell the Committee that the club could use its planning permission to put permanent residential cabins on the land. I know about greed, and I know about human nature. I know that what one gets, the others will soon also want. And I know that if the opportunity arises someone will take it, even if it is at the expense of others. That's one reason why we have a system of planning control in this country, but of course - right now, here, within the confines of the club - we really don't. It's every man and woman for themselves, and nobody – including Zoe – is going to stand up to the Committee and say 'Stop it you idiots. Enough is enough. Can't you see we're destroying the surroundings we all cherish?"*

For just a couple of minutes Leanne not only understood what her husband was thinking about but also why it so concerned him. She suddenly realised that those new cart lodges would mean more trees would have to be cut down, and that a second row of cabins would mean another driveway from the car park would be needed sooner or later. She also realised that her own actions in condemning a healthy willow and an alder to an appointment with Bill's chainsaw had contributed to that destruction.

'Come on,' Leanne said once she'd finally managed to put some uncomfortable pangs of guilt to the back of her mind. 'Let's go and find your mother and father.'

Brad and Leanne left Bill to continue with any pre-planned desecration the Committee had authorised, and went off to deliver Gwen's prescription. Brad tried his best not to get too upset by the sight of a new driveway that had sliced through a small copse, and even managed a brief smile when he spotted a metal sign – clearly purloined from its original location on a new housing development – proudly proclaiming the second row of residences as 'Berkeley Avenue.' Such minor amusement didn't however compensate for the sight of a bare patch of soil that had, until the previous day, been occupied by fifteen metres of mature mixed-species hedgerow. The hedgerow hadn't been covered by the Tree Preservation Order, a fact that both Brad and Zoe had known full well, and which had undoubtedly contributed to its demise. On her previous visits to the club Leanne would have recognised removal of the hedgerow only as providing a new and rather convenient shortcut, but today she recognised it as an important part of the site's natural and rapidly diminishing environment. Unfortunately Leanne didn't recognise a large pile of deer droppings on the surface of the newly exposed soil, and by the time she'd realised what had happened the tractor-treads on the underside of her left trainer were well and truly clogged up. Cursing her misfortunate Leanne let Brad go on ahead to their log cabin, while she proceeded to try and find a stick to remove of much of the mess as she could.

Just as when he'd turned up at his parents' bungalow on the day of Leanne's salt poisoning it didn't appear as if George and Gwen were in residence, so Brad opened the log cabin's front door and went in. On this occasion, however, Brad had been mistaken and he entered the cabin only to find his mother and father curled up in bed under a lightweight duvet. To one side of the bed Brad noticed a pile of black nylon straps with metal buckles and some webbing. He was just wondering what the hell it was and why it was there when his father spoke.

'You might have bloody well knocked,' George complained, as he awoke from a light sleep to find his son standing close to the bed. 'A couple of minutes earlier and you'd have caught the pair of us *en flagrante*.'

'Well don't worry about that now George,' said Gwen, as she waved to Brad. 'You've had more than enough for one day, and to be honest dear I've had more than enough for the whole week. Kissee kissee Bradley dear.'

Just as he had when he'd inadvertently overheard his parents engaged in a close encounter over the phone Brad didn't know what to do or say. His initial disgust at the idea of his parents canoodling – in fact the very thought of it almost made him feel ill – gave way to anger that George should continue to feel the need to satisfy his unnaturally high level of carnal desires with his poorly wife.

'Honestly,' he said 'How could you?'

'It's quite easy dear,' replied Gwen 'First I just make sure George's thingy is nice and sti..'

'I know *how* Mother, what I meant is *why*.'

'Well possibly because we both rather like it dear. Is that a good enough answer for you?'

'Well, not really, no. What I mean is.. Look, are you sure you're well enough to be doing that sort of thing?'

'What sort of thing?' asked Leanne as she entered the cabin, having finally managed to get most of the mess off the underside of her trainers. 'My shoes collected a pile of deer poo so I've left them outside.'

'Thank you dear,' replied Gwen. 'Deer doo-doo is such a devil of a job to get off a carpet.'

'Mother and Father were 'otherwise occupied' just before we arrived,' explained Brad. 'And they were just sleeping it off.'

'And my dear son Bradley was concerned I might not be up to it,' said Gwen, and she gently squeezed her son's arm. 'He *even* asked us how we did it. Fancy not knowing that at his age. Honestly, I ask you. Anyway, I told him that the first thing I do is make sure George's thingy is nice and..'

'He probably asked you that because he's forgotten how to,' replied Leanne. 'But anyway don't worry about that Gwen. Now, I've got your prescription here, but it's just for some Amoxicillin. Is that correct?'

Gwen took the bag from Leanne, opened it and removed the single small box of tablets.

'I suppose those are the right ones dear, I really don't know what they're called.'

'There's no painkillers or anything like that. Just a course of antibiotics.'

'Why would I want painkillers dear?' asked Gwen, as she swung her legs out of the bed and got to her feet.

'For your illness Gwen,' replied Leanne, subconsciously omitting to make any reference to the 'C' word lest it should suddenly become contagious as a result.

'I'm not in any pain dear and it doesn't really hurt, not as such. It just itches a bit, that's all.'

'Itches? What itches?'

'The horrible flaky skin between my toes. I tried rubbing butter onto it, then olive oil, and finally a bit of Vaseline but it didn't help. I was going to try a little baby oil, but we hadn't got much left, and what we had George said he'd got another use for, didn't you dear?'

George nodded but mercifully avoided telling Brad and Leanne precisely what use he had in mind.

'Anyway when none of those worked I went to see Dr Raja, and he told me I'd got a skin infection. I'd finished off the tablets he'd given me but the itching wasn't getting any better so I went back to see Dr Raja again and he gave me a second prescription.'

'But what about your other illness?'

Gwen scratched her head for a couple of seconds and looked pensive.

'I don't think I've got any other illnesses dear. In fact I'm feeling as fit as a fiddle these days. I think staying in your log cabin has helped me no end - and I must say a big 'Thank You' for that —but, as I tell people, I put my youthful zest for life down to a good diet, sensible shoes and the love of a good man despite his frequently excessive demands in the bedroom department.'

'She's right you know,' said George. 'Staying here has helped the old love life no end. We've been having a right old time, haven't we Gwen? The old pork swordsman's getting a bit sore if the truth be told.'

Gwen giggled. 'Really dear. What a thing to say in front of your son and daughter-in-law, particularly in view of his little problem. But yes, it's true, we have. We've been up to all sorts of things, in fact some of them we've never tried before in all these years of marriage. Can you believe that? The thing we tried with the harness yesterday for example. My goodness that *was* fun. We'll have to do that again, but next time we'll have to do the straps up a little tighter. After all George, we don't want you falling out again do we?'

Brad stared at pile of straps and webbing at the side of the bed, and immediately realised what it was for, and also why the ceiling timbers had needed strengthening the other week. Leanne, on the other hand, was more concerned with other matters.

'Gwen, are you saying there's *nothing else* wrong with you?'

'Not that I'm aware of dear, no.'

'So you haven't got cancer?'

'Cancer? No dear. Why, what a strange thing to say.'

'And you've never had it?'

'No dear, never.'

'Oh that is *such* a relief,' exclaimed Brad, giving his mother a big hug. 'That's wonderful news, isn't it Leanne? I'm *so, so* glad.'

Leanne agreed that it was indeed wonderful news, although her assessment appeared to be qualified to the extent that the news was wonderful for Gwen and of course for George, but rather less for her.

'I,' said Leanne, in a tone Brad immediately recognised as not being favourably inclined towards her mother-in-law. 'I have had my arse frozen off camping in a sodding tent, and then ended up lying flat on my back – stark naked – in a foul river of shit and piss when I should have been engulfed in pure orgasmic ecstasy. Then I was nearly poisoned by your fucking salt and pepper sandwiches *and* – *and* – I was denied the relaxation prescribed by Dr Raja as possibly the best cure for my husband's permanent limp. And now *you* - yes *you*, you wicked old woman – are telling me there's *nothing fucking well wrong with you?*'

'What's all this about you being engulfed in orgasmic ecstasy?' asked George before Gwen could reply to Leanne's outburst. 'That's wasn't going to be with our Brad, that's for sure. Fantasising about your perfect man were you?'

'Shut up George, that's *none* of your bloody business. I'm just saying that I was denied something that should be every woman's God-given right, and it must be God-given because if he won't give it to me I'm damned if I know who will - and don't even *think* about volunteering *your* services. And all this because *that* mad old bat..' Leanne pointed to Gwen. '*That* mad old bat made up some fucking cock and bull story and told us she was terminally ill.'

There was a stunned silence in the room and although Gwen glared at her daughter in law with a look that could have sliced through plate steel, she said nothing. Finally Brad broke the deadlock as he recalled what Gwen had actually said.

'She didn't,' he said, quietly.

'*What?*'

'Mother didn't tell us she had cancer.'

'Oh yes she bloody well did!'

'No Leanne, she *didn't*. She told us she'd been to see Dr Raja, but she couldn't remember what he'd told her she'd got. All she could remember was that it began with the letter 'C'. Then, while Mother was telling us what Dr Raja had said, Tina was busy spelling the signs of the zodiac, and had just got to the sign 'Cancer'. Mother never actually *said* what she'd got wrong with her, did you? She knew it began with a 'C' but she never actually said what it was.'

Gwen nodded her head.

'So exactly what the bloody hell *had* you got wrong with you then?' demanded Leanne.

'Cystitis,' replied Gwen, who was clearly most annoyed with Leanne for the way she'd suggested Gwen had misled her family.

'And damn painful it was too. It felt just like I was peeing razor blades. Horrible it was, absolutely horrible.'

'You *told* Brad it was inoperable!' shouted Leanne.

'It *is* inoperable. Have you ever known anyone have an operation for it? No, of course you haven't.'

'You also told us Dr Raja had said *nature would have to take its course!*'

'He most certainly *did!* He *said* the infection would probably clear itself up in a few days and there wasn't any need to prescribe antibiotics. He thought I'd had it almost a fortnight by the time I saw him, which I'm sure I had judging by the number of times I'd been sitting on the lavvy with my fists clenched.'

'So *just how bloody long* was it before you were cured?' demanded Leanne who was becoming increasingly worked up about what she was hearing.

'Oh, a couple of weeks. I think it would have cleared up sooner if I'd been given antibiotics in the first place, but Dr Raja seemed very reluctant to prescribe any. He kept saying the National Health Service had run out of money, and that if he prescribed them for me then one day they might not work for somebody else. That would be awful don't you think? No I don't suppose you would, you selfish, selfish woman – You'd be too busy thinking about yourself, wouldn't you?'

Despite citing Dr Raja's concerns about the potential emergence of superbugs, Leanne remained totally unconvinced that her mother-in-law's explanation justified denying her of some quality time in what was, after all, her log cabin. She didn't answer Gwen's question but instead turned angrily on her father-in-law who had just got out of bed.

'So all this time the pair of you,' – Leanne pointed an accusing finger at George. 'You and her have been happily using our log cabin on false pretences, and fornicating away in here to your hearts' content. Well, let me tell you something, the pair of you - you wicked, wicked old buggers – you can fucking well shift your arses out of here first thing tomorrow morning.'

'You *said* we could have it for as long as we needed it,' replied Gwen, who clearly saw no immediate reason to vacate the premises and had no intention of making any concessions to her daughter-in-law, particularly after the way she'd just been spoken to.

'I *meant* you could have it until you were *dead*.'

'Exactly, and I'm *not*, which should be fairly obvious even to someone as stupid as you. So we're *keeping* it, after all we're paying for it.'

'She's right you know,' replied George, before Leanne had a chance to tell Gwen her demise could easily be arranged, and would she just like to follow her into the woods because she'd suddenly remembered where she'd left a large stick with a wickedly sharpened end. 'We've paid to stay here, haven't we Gwen?'

Gwen nodded her head.

'You're only paying the club its daily camping fee,' said Brad. 'So all you have to do is simply stop paying it and then move out. It's perfectly simple.'

'Actually it's not quite as straightforward as that,' said George. 'Do you remember what I told you about when I was out in Malaya? It was that time me and some of the lads off the ship went to Mr Patel's Passion Parlour and..'

'Father, this is not the time or place to start telling one of your far –fetched tales about Mr Patel and that wretched knocking shop of his. In fact there's never a time or place, but now's especially not it.'

'I was *going* to tell you about the first time we ever went there, and I had that argument with Mr Patel and he called me 'Tight English' because I wouldn't pay him what he wanted for a night's unbridled passion with a couple of his gorgeous young lovelies.'

'So what?'

'So we argued and swore at each other, but eventually we made a deal.'

'A bit like now,' replied Leanne, whose face was becoming increasingly red and her expression increasingly one of exasperation. 'Except that I haven't actually sworn at *you* yet George. So if it helps clarify the situation I'm telling you right here and now that I want the pair of you scheming old buggers to get the fuck out of my log cabin, and pronto. How's that for a deal?'

'No Leanne, that's not any kind of a deal. And even if it was it wouldn't be you I'd be making it with. In fact a deal's already been done with Derek.'

'What the hell do you mean 'with Derek',' asked Brad, the idea of any deal with Derek sounding distinctly ominous. 'Exactly what kind of a deal have you made with Derek?'

'Your mother and I have been paying the club its daily camping fee, but that was becoming expensive bearing in mind how often we were staying here. So I had a word with Derek.'

'And?'

'And I upgraded our membership from 'Silver' to 'Gold'. That, as you will know if you've read the club's constitution, allows your mother and me unlimited camping, although on the down side I've got to clean the damn bogs next Sunday.'

'I don't see how that makes any difference,' said Brad although he didn't get the chance to pursue the argument because Leanne made her position perfectly clear.

'It's *my* bloody cabin and *I want it back,* and that's all there is to it!'

Her final position on the matter made clear Leanne decided she would contribute nothing more to the discussion and stormed out of the cabin, leaving Brad to continue any further negotiations on his own.

'She can *have* it back, the miserable little cow,' said Gwen just as Leanne had slammed the door with a force so great Brad was convinced she'd wrenched it off its hinges. 'She can *have* the log cabin back, can't she George?'

'Yes dear she certainly can. After all, as you say – it's their cabin. The problem is that it's on *our* pitch. And it'll be *our* pitch next year too as far as I'm concerned. Now then Bradley, if you'll just let me explain – What I was *going* to say before I was so rudely interrupted was that when I was arguing with Mr Patel I eventually came up with the idea of 'Buy one, get one free' – BOGOF. I was trying to persuade those miserable shopkeepers to pay me for using the idea without my permission *if* you recall. Anyway, Derek wanted us to pay the 'Gold' fee for the whole summer season, so I told him he was a tight bastard and he said yes, he already knew that. So then I told him I'd only pay the full year's fee if he repaid us what we'd already paid in daily camping fees. He said he couldn't do that because it would upset his cash flow, so I told him he really was as tight as a duck's arse, and he said yes, he knew that as well.'

'Exactly *where* is this getting us Father?' demanded Brad, who was also becoming increasingly annoyed with his parents' seemingly endless waffle.

'Patience, patience. I'll get to it eventually. Right then - Having got nowhere with Derek so far I played my BOGOF Ace. I told him I'd pay the full fee for the rest of this summer, and in return he can give us next year's camping for free. I hate the phrase but it was a 'win-win' situation. We won because we got a summer's camping for free, and Derek won because he got a year's fee in advance. But Derek also reckons he can get a year's fee from the pair of you because he thinks Gwen's going to be six foot under by the end of the year. So that's why he did the deal. He's not entirely stupid after all. But you're not going to be six foot under by then, are you Gwen dear?'

Gwen turned her head to look at George, and then she took his hand in hers and squeezed it tightly.

'Absolutely not George, my darling. I'm feeling as fit as a fiddle. As I tell people, I put my youthful zest for life down to good shoes and a sensible diet – or was it a good diet and sensible shoes? It's one or the other. Oh, and the love of my good man of course – that's you George in case you were wondering – notwithstanding your excessive activity in the bedroom department on more occasions than I care to remember. But as far as that log cabin is concerned Bradley, I'm afraid the bottom line is that my dear George and I want to carry on staying on this lovely site overlooking the lake until the end of next summer at least. After all, you made us an offer and we accepted in it good faith, didn't we George?'

'You also strengthened the roof so you could fit that bloody harness,' replied Brad, and he stared at the pile of black webbing at the side of the bed.

'We'd leave that in the cabin for you if you want,' replied George. 'Call it 'fixtures and fittings' if you like, although it might be bit worn out by then. You might want to try one out for yourself in the meantime - after all with your condition anything's worth a go to see if things can't get moving. They come with a free expansion kit, so if you and Leanne fancy seeing if you can get that Zoe involved in a *ménage a trois* you just need to check that the rafters are man enough for the job. I reckon she'd be up for it if you have a quiet word with her.'

'I'm doing nothing of the sort Father!' exclaimed Brad. 'I'm one hundred per cent behind Leanne on the situation – she's already made it quite clear that we want the cabin back, and that's also my final word on the matter.'

'I see,' said Gwen. 'Well, in that case all you have to do is to arrange for a large crane to come and pick it up and take it off our pitch. Yes Bradley, you heard me. Just get a man with a great big crane to come over here and pick the cabin up, although quite where you're going to put it is another matter because all the lakeside sites are taken, as I believe are all those in the second row. I understand from Derek that the Committee are looking into the possibility of putting in a *third* row, although they won't have views of the lake. Do you know where they're proposing to put them George?'

'Just to one side of the car park and to the left of the toilet block as far as I know,' replied George. 'So at least you'd be able to keep an eye on your car, and the lavvy would be nice and handy when you need it. It's a right pain in the arse having to walk across to the shower block at three o'clock in the morning when all you need a quick Jimmy. In fact that was why some of us wanted a thunder box just behind the first row of cabins. That was the plan, but then some of those miserable buggers in Berkeley Avenue objected, saying it'd be too close to them so we decided to get a proper toilet block built that we could all use. If everything goes to plan they'll be putting it at the back of the holiday cabin so none of the club's members will be affected. There are a few scruffy old trees that'll need taking out but that shouldn't be too much of a problem. Most of them have probably got that honey fungus thing anyway.'

Brad had heard enough. There really wasn't much point arguing with his parents because it was almost inevitable he'd lose, even if he was holding the moral high ground. So in order to avoid further unpleasantness, or possibly even bloodshed if Leanne were to return while the argument was still raging, Brad just said "We'll see about this," and walked out of the cabin, slamming the door behind him. In hindsight he wished he hadn't done that, because his earlier thoughts about the way Leanne had treated the woodwork proved to be correct, resulting in another minor maintenance job if and when the cabin was ever returned to its rightful owners. One of those rightful owners now found himself at odds with his parents about the future occupation of a log cabin while the other one was nowhere to be seen. That was because she'd taken the car keys when she'd stormed off and was now almost back home, where she'd every intention of opening a bottle of wine and a large bar of dark chocolate, finding that set of spare batteries and running herself a hot bath. How long it would take for her husband to walk home, and whether or not he knew where the spare house keys were kept she couldn't give a tinker's cuss.

# Chapter 35

The waters of the lake from which the Hidden Lake Sun Club took its name glistened in the bright summer sun, making Brad squint as he walked away from the log cabin and down to the water's edge. Once his eyes had eventually become accustomed to the intensity of the light Brad started to look around. The willow and silver birch which had lined the water's edge not so many months ago were now almost all gone as were most of the trees behind them, leaving ugly patches of scrubby undergrowth and bracken in their wake. Elsewhere patches of bare earth were beginning to appear, eroded by the heavy summer rainfall which was already beginning to wash the topsoil down into the lake itself. Brad looked around and noticed he could see several cars over in the club's car park. There had never been a clear view of the car park from the lake's edge as far as Brad could recall, leaving him to conclude that even more trees of the 'dead, dying or dangerous' variety must have already been removed to accommodate that proposed third row of log cabins, or mobile homes, or whatever the hell the club's Committee eventually decided they were going to put there. The metal sign proclaiming the second row of cabins as 'Berkeley Avenue' had clearly convinced the occupiers of the first row that they required a similar structure, although the sign had not yet been painted, and the concrete securing it in place had not yet set hard. Perhaps that new sign had also convinced the occupiers of Berkeley Avenue that they needed to keep one step ahead of their neighbours, because the next thing Brad noticed was a row of lamps attached to several three-metre high poles strung out along the side of the new driveway from the car park. Even the driveway appeared to be acting as some kind of catalyst to the development of a number of new cart lodges, although their owners may also have been prompted by Derek's decision that he really couldn't survive without one. In fact everywhere Brad looked he saw change, and change for the worse as far as he was concerned. The loss of so many trees appeared to have caused the occupiers of some log cabins to conclude they didn't have sufficient privacy from their new neighbours, prompting them to put up ugly close-boarded fences that now all but surrounded three side of the cabins - although never the side facing the lake with its wonderful views across the shimmering water. Those views had to be preserved at all costs, but for the benefit of the occupiers of the log cabins alone, or so it appeared.

The more he looked at it the more Brad became convinced the club's once tranquil, wooded grounds would eventually become a naked suburbia for those who could afford one of the increasingly gaudy residences that appeared to be popping up all over the place. It was bad enough that the club's woodland was being lost to a seemingly never ending number of log cabins, but now those cabins seemed to be surrounded by fences, each seemed to have its own cart lodge or pre-fabricated garage complete with a small patch of grass or suburban garden. Even those new gardens couldn't have been more different to the woodland they'd destroyed by their creation. Each had been planted with exotic, ornamental shrubs and other plants that had no place in an English woodland, and each had a length of plastic washing line strung between two metal poles where once a couple of yards of communal string tied between two trees had served the same purpose. The sight of newly constructed trellises, pergolas and rustic arches only added to Brad's dismay, and quite why one cabin in three needed a six foot plastic trampoline in its garden Brad simply couldn't comprehend. Even outside the confines of the two metre close-boarded 'fuck off and mind your own business' fences the club's grounds had changed beyond recognition. Driveways now led from the club's enlarged car park to each of the log cabins, and a few of the cabins even had additional areas of hardstanding to accommodate extra parking. It would surely only be a matter of time before the others acquired similar, and a further area of the club's former woods would be lost beneath concrete and tarmac. There was no doubt about it, the genie was well and truly out of the bottle labelled 'desirable holiday home' and wasn't going to take kindly to being put back inside.

Resigned to the inevitable Brad turned to face the lake once again, but as he did something caught his eye. Beneath the wooden stake that one of the club's members had risked life and limb to secure in place - and which Gwen's kingfisher had last been seen to use as a perch - Brad spotted a small object floating in the water. The vivid electric blue feathers may have become discoloured, but even before he'd fished the poor bird out of the water Brad realised the lifeless animal he'd seen floating in the lake was none other than the kingfisher. Brad had no idea how long the bird had been dead, or why it had died, but as he looked he spotted a small piece of wire protruding from the side of the bird's beak. Perhaps the wire had got trapped in the kingfisher's airway and choked it? Or perhaps it had prevented it from feeding, and the poor thing had simply starved to death. The most likely explanation appeared to be that a careless individual had dropped the wire in the water and the kingfisher had mistaken the shiny nickel coating on the wire for food. After all, the wire was only a couple of inches in length, and when viewed from a branch in a willow tree must have looked just like a small fish. Whatever the actual cause of death Brad couldn't be sure, although he was in no doubt that the source of the wire was the new street lighting in Berkeley Avenue. It was a ridiculous thing to even contemplate, but somehow Brad felt complicit in the kingfisher's death, and for that matter the destruction of the club's woodlands. After all, it was he who had got the club its planning permission in the first place. No, that was a ridiculous thing to think. Brad had got the club that permission at the club's request, but it was the club's members – and in particular its' Committee – who had taken advantage of it for their personal benefit, and had screwed up the club's most important and irreplaceable asset as a result. Whoever was to blame for the kingfisher's demise Brad knew he had to dispose of the animal in a proper and dignified manner, and not by tossing it back into the lake as some would have done. Brad looked around where he was standing and spotted a patch of bracken not a few yards away, so he walked over to the bracken and tore off a handful. Then he walked back to the water's edge where he carefully wrapped the bracken loosely around the kingfisher's lifeless body. But now what? Bury it? And if so, where? Not in any of the cabins' manicured gardens that was for sure, nor in the few remaining communal areas of lawn on the basis that sooner or later they'd be dug up or concreted over. The only place Brad could think of was in the woods, but even then the poor bird would most probably be dug up by a fox, assuming they hadn't already been seen off by the cabin owners' numerous pet cats who would waste no time in digging it up themselves. So Brad didn't bury the kingfisher. As he was pondering exactly what to do - and far less where the hell Leanne was or even which way she might have been heading when she stormed out of the cabin

– Brad noticed a thin plume of smoke coming from what had once been the far side of the club's woods. Immediately he knew what he had to do, and within no more than five minutes he was standing next to a small bonfire which a person or persons unknown had lit to dispose of an unwanted packing crate. The fire was still well alight, so Brad placed the bracken-clad corpse into the fire as gently as he could without getting his hands burnt.

Brad had done what he felt he had to do. Somehow that kingfisher seemed to epitomise everything he'd seen these last few weeks. It had also made his mind up for him. Gwen and George could keep the damn log cabin. And they could keep the pitch to go with it. Westlands was at least ten miles further to drive but at least they didn't have any log cabins, caravans or even planning permission to develop their site. After all, it wasn't as if Brad and Leanne didn't know any of their members. In fact at least half their members had previously belonged to the Hidden Lake Club, but had got well and truly pissed off when the whole debacle of who should be allowed to have a log cabin had started. The membership fees were lower too and everyone, but everyone, shared the toilet cleaning rota.

# Chapter 36

It was at least six weeks since Brad had last visited the Hidden Lake Club. Since that visit - when he'd argued with George and Gwen about the log cabin and ownership of the camping pitch - he and Leanne had discussed joining Westlands, and resigning from the Hidden Lake Club. They'd even downloaded the application form, although they'd never actually got around to completing it or making two mandatory visits under 'naturist conditions' to convince the club that they were *bona fide* naturists and not just out to gawp at some naked flesh. It wasn't that they hadn't really intended to join Westlands -far from it - but events had conspired against them because in addition to Brad still needing to sort out a few things following an unexpected bereavement, he and Leanne had found themselves acting as Agony Aunt and Uncle to Leanne's recently married girlfriend in Newcastle. Just as Brad had predicted the marriage hadn't lasted, although husband number three had remained in the land of the living by running off to Dubai with a Bulgarian lap dancer, having previously transferred the contents of the marital bank account to somewhere in Switzerland. One weekend in Newcastle listening to Leanne's friend Lorraine endlessly wailing Brad could probably have tolerated, but quite why he and Leanne had to go and comfort the wretched gold-digger on two consecutive weekends he couldn't quite figure out. To make matters worse the Hidden Lake Club had been bathed in gloriously warm late summer sunshine on both those weekends, whereas in Newcastle it had remained cloudy and the temperature had just about reached double figures – a situation the Geordies considered almost tropical. On the third weekend the weather in Newcastle appeared to have followed Brad and Leanne back home, and to make matters worse it had rained almost continuously ever since - conditions which were less than ideal for a visit to a naturist club, and also for an important task Brad needed to carry out.

When the rain eventually stopped and the temperature reached the upper-teens Brad got his pushbike out of the garden shed, packed a small rucksack and made his way to the Hidden Lake Club. He'd normally have driven over, but Leanne had taken the car up to Newcastle to see Lorraine who had climbed the Tyne Bridge the previous weekend, and had spent three hours sitting up there threatening to jump off unless her soon-to-be ex-husband could be convinced to transfer half the funds in his Swiss bank account into one in her name. Leanne had been insistent that she should go and see Lorraine once again, and Brad had been equally insistent that he wasn't going as he had more important things to attend to. Eventually a compromise was reached which involved Leanne working out which way up to hold a map and driving to Newcastle alone, leaving Brad to find out how the cooker, washing machine, vacuum cleaner and iron worked. Quite what state those appliances would be in by the time she returned home Leanne didn't care to think, leaving Brad to wonder precisely the same about their car. And so it was, on a late summer's morning as the sun was starting to burn away a thin mist that had formed overnight, that Brad arrived at the Hidden Lake Club sweating as much as he'd done all summer. As soon as he'd recovered from his exertion Brad made his way to the lake to carry out the task he'd been intending to do for the past few weeks. He'd wanted to visit the spot next to the club's holiday cabin, but to his dismay discovered even that area was now fenced off and accessible only via a locked gate to which he didn't have a key. Brad soon discovered that he wasn't able to gain access to the lake on either side of the holiday cabin either, and for the same reason, although in this case it appeared to be the occupiers of the adjacent cabins who had taken matters into their own hands by restricting access to their camping pitches. In fact the more Brad looked for somewhere to get down to the edge of the lake the more he discovered that access to its waters was now the preserve of a privileged minority who had all but claimed it for themselves. This was not the way the club's founders had meant it to be, that was for sure. The woods and the lake were supposed to be enjoyed by all, but the woods had almost entirely disappeared and the lake was virtually inaccessible without a twelve-month camping permit, or the key to one of the locks on sturdy gates intended to deter casual visitors. To make matters worse none of the occupiers of the cabins appeared to be in residence, a fact Brad only discovered when he found Bill working on the roof of a new cart lodge close to the second row of cabins.

'I need to get down the lake,' Brad shouted just as soon as he'd gained Bill's attention.

'You might be able to get down over there if you're careful,' replied Bill, and he pointed over to Brad's left. 'We haven't seen much of you and Leanne recently. Things all right with you?'

Brad didn't answer Bill's question directly but nodded, then waved his hand and started walking towards the cabin furthest away. It was only a couple of minutes' walk along a newly surfaced driveway, and Brad soon found himself gingerly making his way through a patch of waist-high nettles on the far side of a tall fence that marked out the end of civilisation as the cabin's occupiers knew it. The ground beneath his feet was thoroughly sodden and Brad's shoes were soon covered in mud and letting in water, but eventually Brad found himself standing at the very edge of the lake. For all that had gone on at the club in recent months the view across the lake remained unchanged, and that was probably because the club's members hadn't been able to bugger about with it. With a heavy heart Brad spent a couple of minutes admiring the view. The leaves on the few remaining trees were slowly turning red and gold and purple in the hazy sunshine, while the thin mist that had clung to Brad's shirt leaving it damp both inside and out was still hanging over the lake's tranquil waters. It was as close to the perfect spot as Brad was going to get, and he knew as much, so he took a small wooden box out his rucksack and started to remove the lid. He was just about to take the lid off completely when he noticed something out of the corner of his eye. Brad stood perfectly still, just turning his head slowly to see if he could get a better view. There was no doubt about it, no doubt whatsoever. On a thin branch of the only remaining willow tree, not six inches above the surface of the water, a young kingfisher sat keeping watch over its territory. Had the bird noticed Brad? Brad couldn't be sure, but it had just moved its head and now seemed to be watching him as intently as he was watching it. Barely daring to move in case he startled the bird Brad slowly removed the lid from the box and reached out so that his arm was over the edge of the lake. He tilted the box and a light grey powder started to trickle out before becoming a cascade, swirling gently in the lightest of breezes before falling onto the water. It was a symbolic act - Brad knew that - but for all that had happened over the past few months, for good or for bad, this seemed to be the perfect moment. Ashes to ashes, dust to dust. Gwen would have liked that.

**The End.**

**Footnote**

The author wishes to point out that the character 'Brad' is entirely fictitious, and is in no way based on any other person or persons, and specifically not the author himself who does not suffer whatsoever from Brad's affliction, never has and hopefully never will. Last Thursday night was just a one off, is that clear? Good, no more need be said about it then…

# Glossary of Terms

**A4** – An ISO standard paper size of 8.3 x 11.7 inches.

**A12** – The main east coast highway serving Essex and Suffolk. (Extraordinarily, even in 2017 parts of the A12 in north Suffolk are still single carriageway)

**Amoxicillin** - An antibiotic used in the treatment of bacterial infections.

**'Bogs'** – Toilets (slang).

**B&Q** – A major retailer specialising in home improvements, furnishing and DIY.

**'Boozer'** – A drinking establishment, typically a public house (slang).

**Caravan** – In the context of this novel a 'Caravan' refers to the legal definition set out in UK legislation. Originally defined at Section 29 (1) of the Caravan Sites and Control of Development Act 1960 as:

"Any structure designed or adapted for human habitation which is capable of being moved from one place to another (whether being towed, or by being transported on a motor vehicle or trailer) and any motor vehicle so designed or adapted but does not include any railway rolling stock which is for the time being on rails forming part of a system, or any tent."

The definition has subsequently been amended to accommodate twin-unit caravans and also includes limits on the size and height. As a result of the definition structures such as 'log cabins' and 'mobile homes' may also technically be classed as 'Caravans' provided they meet the criteria set out in the legislation. (In the novel this peculiarity of English planning law forms the basis of the argument between Brad and Zoe)


**Chelmsford** – A city and county town of Essex, England. Located approximately 30 miles north-east of London. The towns/cities of Chelmsford in Massachusetts, Ontario and New Brunswick are named after the city.

**'Cock and Bull'** - An implausible story, frequently used as an explanation or excuse. (e.g. - He came up with a cock and bull story to explain why he was late for work)

**'Cock Up' (to)** – Something badly or incorrectly done (slang).

**Councillors** – Persons elected to serve on a Council, in the case of this book the fictitious Two Valleys District Council.

**County Council** – The second level of Government in those parts of the United Kingdom having a three-tier structure.

**District Council** – The Third tier of Government in the United Kingdom (in those areas were a three tier system exists), beneath the County Council (see above). Generally responsible for housing, refuse collection, planning, building control and environmental health matters such as food hygiene and noise nuisance.

**Doncaster** - A large market town in South Yorkshire, England.

**DIY** – 'Do It Yourself', normally used in the context of decorating, repairs etc.

**East Anglia** – The part of Eastern England that projects into the North Sea. It has no defined boundaries but is generally understood to mean the counties of Norfolk, Suffolk and Cambridgeshire, and parts of Essex.

**Essex** – A County in south-east England, bordering London to the south and Suffolk to the north. Largely urban in the south close to London, but rural in the north.

**Geordie** – A native of the city of Newcastle in the north-east of England. Also refers to their distinctive accent.

**G&T –** Gin and tonic

**'Give a toss' (Not To)** – Not to care, not to give a damn (slang).

**HRT** – Hormone Replacement Therapy.

**'Hunky Dory'** – satisfactory, good (slang).

**IBS** – Irritable Bowel Syndrome.

**Ingatestone** – A small town in Essex, England, close to the A12 highway. Within an area of Metropolitan Green Belt land approximately 20 miles north-east of London.

**'Jimmy' (To have a)** = Jimmy riddle = Tiddle = To urinate – Cockney rhyming slang.

**'Knackered' (to be)** – Broken. Also meaning to be tired (I'm knackered) (slang)

**Lavatorium** – In the context of the book a gentlemen's lavatory. Historically the communal washing area in a monastery.

**'Leg Over' (to get one's)** – To have sex (slang).

**Malaya** – The Malay peninsula and parts of the island of Borneo, now known as Malaysia.

**Ménage a trois** – A sexual liaison involving three persons (French)

**Miniten** – A racket sport having similar rules to tennis, but played on a smaller court, and with a wooden bat called a 'thug'. Played exclusively by naturists. Never really likely to be an Olympic sport…

**'Monkey' (A)** – £500 (Five Hundred Pounds Sterling) (slang).

**'Nick nacks'** – Typically small, worthless. household objects.

**Newcastle (upon Tyne)** – A city in Tyne and Wear, North East England, approximately 270 miles north of London, and located on the north bank of the River Tyne.

**NHS** – National Health Service.

**Nyotaimori** - The Japanese practice of serving food, typically sashimi or sushi, from a woman's naked body.

**PIN** (number) – Personal Identification Number.

**Planning Committee** – A Committee made up of elected Councillors (Members) who are responsible for making decisions on planning and associated applications. The political balance of a Planning Committee at a Council will reflect that of the Council itself.

**Planning Permission** – A permission issued by the relevant authority to develop land (typically by constructing a building or making a change in the use of land).

**QED** – An abbreviation of the Latin phrase *'quod erat demonstrandum'*. Translates as 'which was to be demonstrated.'

**'Quid'** – A slang term meaning £1 (One Pound Sterling). Five quid is £5.

**Ringgit –** The currency of the Republic of Malaysia.

**'Ruby' –** Ruby Murray = Curry (Cockney rhyming slang). 'A ruby and a pint' = A curry and a pint of beer. Ruby Murray was a popular singer in the 1940s and 1950s, but is now perhaps best remembered by this rhyming slang.

**Septic tank** - A tank, usually underground, in which sewage is collected and allowed to decompose through bacterial activity before draining away.

**'Ship Shape' –** Neat and trim; In good order.

**Site licence –** In the context of the novel a 'Site Licence' refers to a licence required from the Local Council to allow the siting of caravans.

**'Stiffy' –** An erection (slang).

**Stowmarket –** A market town in Suffolk, England, perhaps best known for an explosion in a gun cotton factory in 1871 that killed twenty-four people.

**'Stud muffin'** - A man considered to be sexually attractive, typically one with well-developed muscles.

**Suffolk –** A County in eastern England, bordering Essex to the south and Norfolk to the north. The name derives from its former inhabitants- the 'South Folk' who lived to the south of the Waveney Valley, as distinct from the residents of Norfolk – the 'North Folk.'

**'Tinker's Cuss' -** Not interested in, or worried about, something or someone. Usually applied to something insignificant (e.g. - I don't give a tinker's cuss about what he thinks).

**Thunder Box** – Usually refers to a portable toilet (slang)

**'Tickety boo'** – Fine, okay.

**'Tiddle'** – To urinate (slang).

**Tree Preservation Order** – An Order made by a Local Council (more precisely a Local Planning Authority) to protect trees (individually or in a group or within an area) from deliberate damage or destruction. Such Orders can prohibit felling, lopping, topping, uprooting or other damage without permission. Carrying out works to protected trees without the grant of consent can be a criminal offence punishable by a fine.

**'Willy Nilly'** – Without planning; haphazardly.

**E&OE.**

## Titles by Matthew Black:

## 'CLOTHING OPTIONAL'

The cash-strapped owners of an English country house hotel decide to supplement their meagre income by hiring their swimming pool, sauna and leisure facilities to a naturist club.

### 'OVER EXPOSED'

There's a flasher on the loose and to make matters worse the latest victim is the Police Commissioner's favourite niece. Those crazy nudists have to be to blame, don't they?

## THE 'HIDDEN LAKE SUN CLUB' TETRALOGY:

### Part 1 - 'NINE YEARS NAKED'

Tragedy strikes at the Hidden Lake Sun Club, and things go from very bad to even worse when an 'Open Day' designed to attract new members succeeds only in encouraging those for whom a 'naked lifestyle' means a sexual free for all.

### Part 2 - 'NAKED BUCKET LIST'

A video of a naked grandmother stuck on a zip wire high above the Mexican jungle becomes an Internet sensation.

## Part 3 - 'BODY PARTS'

Eccentric grandmother Gwen Dixon tries every trick to get her son a wife. The problem is he already has one.


## Part 4 - 'SCREW FIRMLY FROM REAR'

Eccentric grandmother Gwen is ill, the Hidden Lake Club is facing a financial crisis and a chance encounter with an old flame raises the possibility of a cure for a gentleman's problem of a *very* personal nature.

36280826R00188

Printed in Great Britain
by Amazon